PROSPECT: I said I'm not interested.

SALESMAN: I understand, Bill. But before I leave, may I ask you a question? You're familiar with the value of the U.S. Patent Office, aren't you?

PROSPECT: Yes, I am. What are you getting at?

SALESMAN: Well, believe it or not, during John Quincy Adams's administration, Congress came within three votes of killing it! Congress believed that all the good ideas had already been patented and wanted to save the taxpayers' money. Since then, of course, we've been deluged with technological inventions: radios, automobiles, television, typewriters, dictating equipment, copying machines, computers, orbiting satellites, and who knows what all, even in your own business. The question I would like to ask before I leave, Bill, is: *Have you closed your patent office?*

PROSPECT: No. Not if you put it that way, Michael.

SALESMAN: Well, sit down for a few minutes and let me show you what's in this briefcase.

THE PERFECT SALES PRESENTATION

THE
PERFECT SALES
PRESENTATION

Robert L. Shook

BANTAM BOOKS
NEW YORK · TORONTO · LONDON · SYDNEY · AUCKLAND

THE PERFECT SALES PRESENTATION
A Bantam Book
Bantam hardcover edition / December 1986
Bantam paperback edition / March 1990

Cover photo credits:
Mary Kay Ash: Francesco Scavullo
Buck Rodgers: Bachrach
Bettye Hardeman: Bern-Art Studio
Joe Gandolfo: Dick Phillips
Martin Shafiroff: David Savatteri
Author photo of Robert L. Shook by David Kopolvic

Library of Congress Cataloging-in-Publication Data

Shook, Robert L., 1938–
    The perfect sales presentation.

    1. Selling.   I. Title.
HF5438.25.S56   1986   658.8′5   86-47566
ISBN 0-553-26637-3

Published simultaneously in the United States and Canada

---

*Bantam Books are published by Bantam Books, a division of Ban-
tam Doubleday Dell Publishing Group, Inc. Its trademark, consisting of the words "Bantam Books" and the portrayal of a rooster, is
Registered in U.S. Patent and Trademark Office and in other
countries. Marca Registrada. Bantam Books, 666 Fifth Avenue,
New York, New York 10103.*

PRINTED IN THE UNITED STATES OF AMERICA

OPM   0 9 8 7 6 5 4 3

To Bettye, Buck, Joe, Marty, and Mary Kay

Without whom the Perfect Sales Presentation
wouldn't have been possible.

In memory of
my brother, Richard R. Shook

Acknowledgments

This book could not have been written without the participation of the five members of the sales experts panel: Mary Kay Ash, Joe Gandolfo, Bettye Hardeman, Buck Rodgers, and Martin Shafiroff. Each devoted many hours of valuable time, giving me full cooperation in my research. I am truly indebted to these dear, wonderful friends.

I am grateful to Jim McEachern, CEO and chairman of the board of Tom James Company, who generously gave me his valuable time and shared his sales knowledge. The Tom James Company's highly professional sales organization also provided me with vital data on the men's clothing industry. And special thanks to Tom James's super salesperson, Naresh Khanna, whom I had the privilege to observe in action when I spent a day in the field with him in Atlanta. And also to Jim Rieser, their representative in Columbus.

My thanks to Warren Cox, Judi Levine, and Mary Liff for their assistance in the preparation of the manuscript.

As usual, my good friend and agent, Al Zuckerman, served as my mentor. I always appreciate his advice. And last but not least, a special thank you to my editor, Linda Cunningham, who insisted that I rewrite a major portion of the manuscript after I thought I was finished. I did, but with reluctance—and when the manuscript was completed, I knew Linda was *so* right.

It's easy to write a good book with the kind of support these wonderful people gave me.

Contents

INTRODUCTION

I spent seventeen years in sales prior to becoming a full-time writer, so I know the importance of getting right to the point.

The purpose of this book is to teach you how to make *The Perfect Sales Presentation*. To anyone who earns his or her livelihood selling, the possession of such a sales presentation is utopian. Imagine being able to apply infallible selling techniques every time you are face-to-face with a prospect. During my selling days I often fantasized about the joy of being equipped with such surefire ammunition—only to dismiss my thoughts as pipedreams. Is perfection ever attainable?

For the record, I never entertained the illusion that I alone could create a *perfect* sales presentation. I think it would be presumptuous for *anyone* to attempt that feat singlehandedly. However, I did believe that such perfection could be approached through the joint efforts of some of the world's greatest salespersons; it would take a combined effort of a group consisting of the top sales experts in five very different fields.

In my search for the ultimate sales presentation, I organized the most distinguished group of sales experts ever assembled. Each of these five people is the best in his or her field. From their combined, varied sales

3

experiences and vast acumen the ideal sales presentation has evolved.

Allow me to introduce the five members of this elite group, some of whom may already be familiar to you:

Mary Kay Ash, chairman and founder of Mary Kay Cosmetics, who heads a direct sales organization of approximately 150,000 saleswomen.

Joe Gandolfo, the world's number one life insurance agent, who has produced sales in excess of $1 billion in a single year.

Bettye Hardeman, America's top real estate agent, whose sales of residential properties in 1985 totaled more than $26.2 million.

Buck Rodgers, marketing consultant and former Senior Vice-President for IBM for ten years, in charge of worldwide marketing of all company products. IBMers call him "Mr. Super Salesman."

Martin Shafiroff, a partner at Shearson Lehman/American Express, Inc., who is the number one stockbroker in the world. His annual commissions for retail sales have exceeded $12 million.

None of these five is what you might call a "flash in the pan." For many years they have all been judged by their peers as outstanding performers in their respective fields. Their records of achievement are well documented. In Part V, each of them is profiled.

I have spent hundreds of hours with these dynamic salespeople, observing them in action in the field as well as conducting extensive tape-recorded interviews. I wasn't satisfied simply to witness the application of their selling skills, watching sale after sale being made. I was also interested in discovering the underlying psychology that made each technique effective. I wanted to know everything: Why did you say that to the receptionist?; What was your purpose in introducing yourself to the prospect the way you did?; Why did you reply to the prospect's objection in that way?; Did you say that to better control the sale?; Are you assuming the closing of a sale when you . . . ? I asked literally thousands of questions in order to reveal the purpose behind every sales technique applied. Frequently I had to draw out the answers I was searching for. Since these salespeople often sold instinctively, they were not always aware of the specific techniques they were employing so effectively and that invariably culminated in a sale. Through careful analysis, however, I was able to determine why the various facets of each presentation generated such predictable success.

Although these five individuals are top salespersons in their respective fields, it was interesting for me to discover that no one of them gives a perfect sales presentation. Each is, of course, a master salesperson in his or her own field and, across the board, exceedingly effective in delivering sales presentations. But, having seen all five of them in action, I observed slight differences among them in the various aspects of selling. One would invariably excel over the others in a particular facet of his or her sales presentation. For example, one was better at setting up appointments; another, at controlling the sale; while another at closing the sale. So *The Perfect Sales Presentation* is a composite, incorporating the most outstanding techniques of the world's masters of salesmanship. Review it. Study it. Dissect it. Emulate it.

You will find *The Perfect Sales Presentation* an action-packed source of selling ideas—regardless of the product you sell. It's a complete sale, presented by a fictional character, Michael Baker, the perfect salesperson. Since absolute perfection can never be attained, the script itself is fictional. However, Baker's sales presentation is real in every meaningful sense of the word. It embodies the best selling techniques of supersalespersons Ash, Gandolfo, Hardeman, Rodgers, and Shafiroff. It is true to life, field tested, and based on actual experiences.

As you read this book, it will become obvious that the application of its selling techniques will vary from reader to reader according to the product he or she sells. For example, a stockbroker is likely to make a complete sale on the telephone, whereas a real estate agent will use the telephone chiefly for setting up appointments and servicing clients. Then, too, a furniture manufacturer's representative who has long-term working relationships with his regular buyers might project a more casual, outgoing personality than will a computer salesperson who is making a formal initial presentation to a group of bankers. This book requires you to do some "creative" reading, therefore, in order to apply its principles specifically to your sales career. But, since creativity is an essential quality of every successful salesperson, you should not find this task insurmountable.

So here's your chance to "ride shotgun" with Michael Baker and observe how he sells with perfection. Not only will you witness him in action firsthand; you will learn in detail everything that's going on *behind the scenes*. For your convenience, an explanation of the entire dialogue between Baker and the prospect is given in regular print beneath the prose that appears in bold print. By understanding the *whys*, you'll be able to adopt many of the sales tips from *The Perfect Sales Presentation*, develop them, and apply them when you are confronting new prospects. As Oliver Wendell Holmes said, "Many times ideas grow better when transplanted from one mind to another." There are no patents on any of the concepts in *The Perfect Sales Presentation*.

As with anything, how much you derive from this book is subject to your initiative and innovation. A wealth of information is available to you. It's up to you to take advantage of it.

PART I
BEFORE THE
PRESENTATION

Getting Organized and Making Appointments

As Michael Baker will demonstrate, there are several things that a salesperson should do *before* making an actual face-to-face presentation. Obviously, an appointment must be made with the prospect (in Baker's case, he has elected to schedule one by telephone). Also, assuming that the salesperson is qualified to make the sales call (being "qualified" means that he or she has acquired the necessary product knowledge, is properly prepared to answer all industry-related questions, and understands the needs of the customer), effective time management is essential to achieve the maximum number of sales presentations each day. Additionally, some basic information about the prospect is necessary; just how much varies from industry to industry. But be prepared—successful selling is dependent on much more than the art of persuasion.

It's Thursday, a little past four o'clock. Michael Baker, age thirty-five, briskly walks into his office. Six feet tall, the dynamic man is dressed immaculately in a dark blue suit. With the exception of a quick lunch, he has been working nonstop since seven. A client who had scheduled an appointment with Baker for four o'clock is unavailable. With a five-thirty appointment remaining

9

on his agenda for today, Baker plans to make use of the "down time" by spending the next forty-five minutes on the phone setting up sales presentations for the following week.

His appointment scheduling and general office work are not routinely done during prime selling time. However, with a broken appointment on his hands, Baker is doing what he considers the second best use of his prime time, with eyeball-to-eyeball sales presentations being in first place by a wide margin.

Seated back at his desk, he takes out several dozen notecards on prospects located in a four-block radius of a commercial area on the northeast side of town; none of the calls is more than a five-minute drive from the others. Each card contains the prospect's name, occupation, address, phone number, and miscellaneous information about how he obtained the lead. To Baker, a "qualified" prospect is an individual who meets certain criteria based on his estimated earnings and vocation. Other considerations include the prospect's age, lifestyle, and special interests. Each prospect card contains the name of the source who gave the referral to Baker—he considers referred prospects his best leads. The majority of his referrals have been generated by his existing clientele. All available pertinent information about the prospect has been jotted down on the card. A nonreferred prospect is an individual whom he knows by reputation in the community through such sources as newspaper articles, the grapevine, and so on. Still other prospects are selected and categorized by occupation.

Under no circumstances does Baker call a prospect without knowing his name in advance. For example, if he wanted to speak with the executive vice-president of manufacturing at XYZ Company but didn't know his name, Baker would make a call a day or so in advance and ask the main switchboard operator or receptionist, "Who is the company's marketing vice-president?" Later, he would put through a call to the individual.

Baker has mapped out his prospects in a small section of town to avoid accumulating a lot of "windshield" time chasing from one side of the city to the other. To accomplish this, he has carefully keyed each call on a map of his territory, soliciting prospects only in a specific area. Relying on the law of averages, he has more than enough names at his fingertips to call during the next forty-five minutes. Knowing he won't have an opportunity to talk to each prospect—some won't be available, others won't be interested, etc.—he attempts to call as many prospects as possible. One of his calls is to William Silver, the chairman of the board of National Manufacturing Corporation.

The Telephone Presentation for an Appointment

MAIN OPERATOR: Good morning, National Manufacturing Corporation.

MICHAEL BAKER: May I please speak to William Silver?

In the initial approach, it's important to have the name of your prospect. In this case, Bill Silver is the chairman of the board. It would have been improper to say, "May I please speak to the company's chairman."

SECRETARY: Good morning, Mr. Silver's office.

BAKER: Good morning. This is Michael Baker. Bill Silver, please.

Baker immediately identifies himself. However, although he has never met the actual prospect, Baker refers to him by his first name, acting as though he knows him personally. As a result, sometimes a secretary will assume Baker is an acquaintance and put the call through. In this case, however, she doesn't.

SECRETARY: Does Mr. Silver know you?

BAKER: **Please tell him this is Michael Baker with Winchester Associates. Is he in?**

Electing not to answer the secretary's question because he doesn't personally know the prospect, Baker identifies himself once again, but this time he states the name of his company. He controls the conversation by asking the secretary a question: "Is he in?" Now she is required to give an answer—she must think of a reply. By doing this, Baker attempts to avoid having *her* question him.

SECRETARY: **Yes. What is the nature of your call?**

She continues to ask questions.

BAKER: **This is Michael Baker with Winchester Associates. Whom am I speaking with, ma'am?**

Not wanting to give her specifics, Baker repeats his name and his company's and again asks a question that requires an answer. He also wants her name for future reference because she will be flattered that he remembered.

SECRETARY: **This is Mary Wilson.**

He jots down her name.

BAKER: **Would you kindly tell Mr. Silver that I'm on the line, Miss Wilson?**

He authoritatively tells her to advise the prospect that he's on the phone. Please note that it's the secretary's job to screen calls—which Baker fully realizes.

SECRETARY: **What is the nature of your call, Mr. Baker?**

BAKER: Miss Wilson, I know what your job entails, and I realize Mr. Silver is a busy person. I also know that it's hard for you to decide whom he speaks to. However, I do have something really worthwhile to discuss with him, and what I have to say will be well worth his time. I'm sure he will appreciate that you gave me a chance to speak with him. Would you please tell him that I'm on the line?

Baker is having an unusually difficult time and again makes an effort to get through to the prospect. However, he realizes that busy people like Silver are not always easy to reach. Still, Baker purposely avoids telling her the exact nature of his call—knowing that she might attempt to explain it to the prospect for him. Baker knows that nobody will tell his story as effectively as he himself will, so he remains persistent.

SECRETARY: One moment please.

Because Baker has spoken with confidence, the secretary elected not to exercise her right to cross-examine him. Had he hemmed and hawed, she might have continued questioning him. His persistence and professionalism win out!

SECRETARY: He's on the telephone. Do you wish to leave a message?

The prospect is not available. Baker must now make a decision whether to leave a message.

BAKER: Thank you very much, Miss Wilson. It's important that I talk to him, so I'll hold.

He decides to wait rather than call back and risk another cross-examination. Also, he doesn't want to leave a message and risk not having the prospect return his call. Baker speaks in a no-nonsense manner and creates a sense of urgency, suggesting that he must talk to Silver now. She puts him on hold and is left with the impression that Michael Baker has something important to talk about with her employer.

SECRETARY: I'll put your call through now, Mr. Baker.

SILVER: Hello.

BAKER: Bill, this is Michael Baker with Winchester Associates. We specialize in fine custom clothing for discriminate business and professional men. You're familiar with Winchester Associates, aren't you?

Baker's opening line states both his name and his company's. Then he immediately states the nature of his business. Note that he gets right to the point. He then asks a question that assumes the prospect knows his company, suggesting that Winchester Associates is a well-known, established company. He controls the interview by asking a yes-or-no question.

SILVER: No. What are you selling?

BAKER: I called to ask for an opportunity to meet with you sometime next week to share an idea with you that has been helpful to many leading businessmen in town. It's an exciting concept that has been well received by our city's top executives at such companies as City National Bank, Western Dynamics, International Foods, and Universal Business Machines. I just need a few minutes of your time to drop by and introduce myself. Would next Tuesday morning at eight-fifteen be convenient, or would two forty-five on Wednesday afternoon be better?

Baker attempts to put the prospect at ease by telling him he wants only to share an idea with him. He explains that other executives in the community have been receptive, and mentions the names of several prominent companies in the area. By giving these names, he implies that influential people are his clients and that the prospect, like them, should be open to a new concept. After all, every astute businessperson should welcome new ideas. Baker gives a choice of two times during the following week for an appointment. He doesn't ask if the prospect will see him, but *when*. Additionally, next week is far enough away that the prospect doesn't feel uncomfortable about committing his time now.

SILVER: How about giving me a call on Monday and I'll let you know.

BAKER: I work only by appointment, Bill. However, I'll be in the area next week. I can see you on Tuesday morning at eight-fifteen or Wednesday afternoon at two forty-five.

Baker establishes the fact that he is a busy person and his time is valuable. Again, he offers a choice of two times.

SILVER: My schedule looks rather hectic next week.

BAKER: Then let's get together before your day gets too hectic, Bill. Would seven or seven-thirty on Tuesday or Wednesday morning be okay?

By asking to see his prospect early in the morning, Baker demonstrates that he is a hardworking individual—a quality that successful people like Silver probably respect and identify with. He believes that by projecting this image, he establishes a rapport with successful people. And, once again, an "either or" choice of times is offered.

SILVER: I'm really not interested, Michael. . . .

BAKER: It will just take a few minutes of your time for me to run some new ideas by you that have been of help to other leading businesspeople in town. If they fit in your philosophy and pocketbook, great. If not, I promise you I'll be on my way. Certainly you have no objections to that, do you?

Instead of giving up when he encounters a negative response, Baker again asks to present some new ideas that have been well received by others. In addition, he states that if the prospect is not interested, he'll be gone quickly, so there is nothing to lose.

SILVER: Mmm, let's see. Make it seven on Tuesday morning.

BAKER: Thank you, Bill. I'm looking forward to meeting you. I'll mark it down in my datebook and see you on Tuesday morning in your office at seven sharp.

Baker thanks the prospect and repeats the time and place for the meeting. By mentioning that he is writing it down in his datebook, he implies that it is a definite appointment—in writing.

Baker's sole objective has been accomplished: he has secured a definite appointment. His telephone presentation was brief and to the point, yet he didn't volunteer too much information. Had the prospect asked specific questions, Baker would have given concise answers and continued his efforts to accomplish his single mission—getting the appointment. Under no circumstances should he have attempted to sell. A professional salesperson *never* gives his sales presentation when a call is made to set up an appointment. This cardinal rule applies also during an in-person call to set up an appointment.

THE TELEPHONE FOLLOW-UP LETTER

After the appointment is made, a brief informal follow-up letter should be sent to the prospect. Here is Michael Baker's standard follow-up letter:

Dear Bill:

It was a pleasure talking to you this afternoon, and I am looking forward to meeting you next Tuesday morning at 7:00.

For your information, I am enclosing some literature about Winchester Associates. As I mentioned this afternoon, we specialize in fine custom-made clothing for discriminate business and professional people, and we cater to an exclusive market; I am sure you are acquainted with many of our clients. Our marketing concept will save you time and money. I welcome the opportunity to share it with you.

Sincerely,
Michael Baker

In addition to confirming the appointment, Baker's concise, courteous letter is relatively low-key. An enclosed company brochure includes full-color illustrations of beautifully displayed Winchester merchandise. The brochure has a brief history of Winchester Associates and includes the company's philosophy about servicing its customers. Additionally, Baker encloses some newspaper and trade-magazine articles about his successful career. For the salesperson who doesn't have an impressive collection of publications about his career, a brief biosketch is appropriate. The biosketch may include one's business philosophy and a few endorsements from respected clients in the area.

In short, Baker has informed his prospect that he is an expert in his business, representing an outstanding company. The prospect has been prepared to meet a professional.

PART II
THE PERFECT
SALES
PRESENTATION

Instructions
to the Reader

Please note that the dialogue between Michael Baker and William Silver appears in bold print. Commentary on all concepts of the sales presentation appears in regular print. This sharp contrast will enable you to read the presentation separately without distraction. It is suggested that you first read the sales presentation in its entirety. Then, read it again with the commentary.

The Presentation

BAKER: **Good morning, Bill. I'm Michael Baker with Winchester Associates. It's a pleasure to meet you.**

Baker enthusiastically introduces himself, stating both his name and the company's. He gives the prospect a firm handshake and begins the conversation on a first-name basis.

SILVER: **It's nice to know you, Michael.**

BAKER: **Your office is magnificent. (pause) Let's sit down at this coffee table and talk, Bill. I have a few things that I want to go over with you as well as show you.**

(walking to a conversation area)

After a sincere, brief compliment, Baker gets right down to business. Taking control, he suggests sitting at the coffee table. Rather than waiting for the prospect to consent, Baker walks to the table, places his briefcase on the floor next to his chair, and sits down. The prospect automatically sits in the chair across from Baker.

BAKER: As you read in the literature I mailed to you, Bill, Winchester Associates specializes in custom-made clothing. We have an elite clientele of business and professional men like yourself—top-flight executives who are very selective, demand fine quality, appreciate outstanding value, and place a high premium on their time. We've been in this business for twenty-four years, and the reception we've had from the business community has been truly exceptional. By and large, our success is due to the unique services we provide for our clients. Today, we have forty-one offices located throughout the United States and Canada. Our last year's sales were $110 million, and we anticipate sales in excess of $150 million this year.

Rather than asking Silver if he read the material, Baker automatically assumes he did, and his opening remarks highlight the nature of the company's business, including its success. Baker wants Silver to know that many other executives have benefited from Winchester's unique services. He states the company's present and projected sales volume to inform the prospect that Winchester is a substantial company; this information informs the prospect that he is dealing with a sizable firm that will be around for a long time. As Baker speaks, he looks his prospect squarely in the eye. His voice is soft, and he speaks slowly and distinctly.

SILVER: I glanced at the brochure you sent me, and there's no need for you to get too comfortable. I appreciate your stopping by, but I'm really very busy.

He stands up abruptly, indicating that Baker shouldn't continue with his sales presentation.

BAKER: Did I catch you at a bad time, Bill? (a brief pause) If so, perhaps we can set up an appointment when you're not so busy.

Baker pays little attention to the prospect's disinterest and feels him out by suggesting he come back at another time. Meanwhile, Baker remains seated. If he were to stand, it would be too easy for the prospect to walk him to the door and bid him farewell.

SILVER: It's not a matter of being too busy to talk to you now, Michael. I'm simply not interested. I'm perfectly happy with my present clothing source.

BAKER: This will only take a few minutes, Bill, and right now I'd just like to run a few ideas by you that have been very helpful to so many other businessmen like yourself in town.

Realizing that he might lose the opportunity to give his presentation, Baker first mentions that he won't take a lot of Silver's time, and then he tries to entice the prospect by offering to share a few new ideas with him—an irresistible opportunity to most successful people. However, Silver again responds negatively.

SILVER: I said I'm not interested, Michael. (abruptly spoken)

BAKER: I understand, Bill. But, before I leave, may I ask you a question? (spoken in a friendly manner)

Baker stands and picks up his briefcase as if to indicate he will leave after he asks one question. By doing this, the prospect drops his guard.

SILVER: Sure, what is it?

BAKER: Bill, as I said, I wanted to share an idea with you. You're familiar with the value of the U.S. Patent Office, aren't you?

SILVER: Yes I am. What are you getting at?

BAKER: Well, believe it or not, during John Quincy Adams's adminstration, Congress came within three votes of killing it! Congress believed that all the good ideas had already been patented, and wanted to save the taxpayers' money. Since then, of course, we've been deluged with technological inventions: radios, automobiles, television, typewriters, dictating equipment, copying machines, computers, orbiting satellites, and who knows what all, even in your own business. The question I would like to ask before I leave, Bill, is: *Have you closed your patent office?*

SILVER: No. Not if you put it that way, Michael.

BAKER: Well, sit down for a few minutes and let me show you what's in this briefcase. I promise that you're going to think this is the greatest thing since sliced bread.

Baker immediately sits down, not waiting for Silver to reply. Again he assumes that the prospect is interested. And while he's ready to get right down to business, he smiles after his sliced-bread comment—to take the edge off an otherwise tense moment.

SILVER: Will this take very long? (hesitating as he sits down)

BAKER: I'm going to review and show you some exciting concepts that have benefited many leading

>businessmen in town, Bill. And if you feel as
>though they meet your needs, fine. If not, I'll
>just be on my way. (spoken matter-of-factly)

This low-key remark tells the prospect, "Listen to
what I have to say. It won't bother me if you don't
buy." Again, the prospect is put at ease.

SILVER: **Okay, let's hear what you have to say. But
I'm not buying today.** (somewhat dropping his
guard)

Finally, after some initial resistance, Baker gets on
the right track, paying no attention to the comment,
"But I'm not buying today." At this stage, his number one mission is to have an audience. It would be
unrealistic to expect a prospect to say, "Let's hear
what you have to say. I'm buying today!" Baker now
feels confident because he has permission to give a
full presentation without the anticipation of continued interruption.

Baker is also aware that Silver has become a prime
prospect. From past experience, he knows that the
more resistance a person gives during the approach,
the less resistance is likely to occur once the presentation is under way. This assumption is based on the
fact that an individual who knows he has difficulty
saying no to salespeople tries to avoid being the
recipient of a sales presentation. Consequently, this
type of prospect permits few salespeople through his
door. Those who manage to get past this initial barrier can expect to experience smooth sailing. Baker
knows that it's worth the extra effort to be persistent
with these prospects. While they listen to fewer
sales presentations, when they do, the chances of
their buying are proportionately higher than other
prospects. For this reason, Baker's confidence level
has justifiably increased.

BAKER: First, Bill, let me begin by saying we provide a very important service for our clients. We cater to a very elite clientele—people such as yourself, who place a high value on their time. For example, just to name a cross-section of a few of our clients whom you may know, Bob Wilson, CEO at National Insurance, has been doing business with us for years. So has Herbert Burnett, the chairman at First Bank, and Richard Carter, who's president at State Bank. Jon Paul at Paul and Company is a client, and so is Al Early, the managing partner at Goodwin Early and Zollinger.

Baker states his first selling point by emphasizing that he can save time for his prospect. He also flatters Silver by stating that his clientele is elite (the assumption is made: "You're elite or I wouldn't be calling on you"). Then, he casually drops some names of important people in town who are clients—men whom Silver probably knows personally or knows about. By mentioning the names of well-respected clients, by innuendo Baker is suggesting: "These intelligent people used good judgment in doing business with us."

SILVER: Yes, I know Herb Burnett well, and I know Jon Paul and Al Early. You named some pretty big hitters.

BAKER: Yes, we do business with some real VIPs. (said matter-of-factly) Like the majority of my clients, you probably have an immense dislike for shopping. First, there's never enough time, and second, when you do have some leisure time, there's probably a zillion other things you'd rather do with it. Don't you agree, Bill?

An advantage of doing business with Baker is that he provides a convenience for the prospect. Baker assumes the answer when he asks, "Don't you agree, Bill?"

SILVER: You're right. I *despise* shopping for clothes! But it's something that can't be avoided.

Silver's voice indicates his dislike for shopping and signals to Baker that he should emphasize this point.

BAKER: What size suit do you wear, Bill? (studying the prospect)

SILVER: I wear a forty-four long.

BAKER: You have broad shoulders and a narrow waist. What size waist do you have?

SILVER: Thirty-five.

BAKER: As you know, there isn't much of a selection of ready-made suits in your size. And when you do find something you like, your waist requires a lot of alterations. Where do you buy your suits now, Bill?

Baker creates an awareness of how few suits are available to the prospect in his size. He asks the name of the prospect's source for suits in order to get a better understanding of his competition.

SILVER: I've been shopping for years at Meyer Brothers.

BAKER: Yes, Meyer Brothers is an excellent store. (said sincerely)

Never knock the competition—either say good things or say nothing at all.

SILVER: I've been very satisfied with them. But, like you say, Michael, I sometimes have a difficult time finding a large selection in my particular size.

BAKER: Actually, Bill, the same thing applies to men who wear common sizes. By the time a well-dressed man eliminates the suits already in his wardrobe, there are only a few suits left to choose still on the rack. In fact, sometimes you have to visit several stores before you can find a suit that really grabs you—again a very time-consuming and tedious chore. With Winchester, I can show four-thousand-plus fabrics and patterns right from my briefcase. But relax, I'm not going to show you all four thousand.

Subtly, Baker mentions a disadvantage that all clothing retailers have in comparison to what he offers.

SILVER: Yeah, shopping around for a specific suit absolutely drives me up a wall.

BAKER: Another advantage we offer is that we can make a suit to fit your exact specifications. For example, you might find a pattern you like at the store, but it's not the ideal weight for you. Or perhaps you want a vest but a particular suit doesn't come with one. Or a suit has two buttons and you want three buttons. Or maybe you want the pants without pleats. Or the jacket with different buttons. There's an endless number of reasons why any given ready-to-wear suit may not fit the bill. I think that when you pay good money for a suit, you should get exactly what you want. Don't you agree?

Here's some food for thought that demonstrates one of the reasons why a tailor-made suit makes a great deal of sense. His "Don't you agree?" question can be answered only affirmatively.

SILVER: Yes, I see what you mean.

BAKER: What price suits do you usually buy?

It's now time for Baker to bring up the subject of price.

SILVER: Generally in the four-hundred-dollar range. What do your suits run?

BAKER: We start at three hundred seventy-five and go up to eight hundred dollars. So, you see, we're in the same ballpark.

Without hesitation, Baker gives a broad price range and doesn't make an issue of it; he then continues with his presentation.

BAKER: Now, what my clients really find convenient is that they can do all of their shopping for suits without ever having to leave their offices. My clients never have to drive through traffic, find a parking space, stand around waiting for a salesclerk, and they don't have to take something back that doesn't fit correctly. I make things very easy for them. I do all the running for them. You know, I really spoil my clients. (a slight pause and a smile) I work by appointment, and I consult with them twice each year, unless, of course, somebody requests to see me in between. I'm only as far away as the telephone. Henry McDonald, with McDonald Public Relations, who's a client of ours, says that I should be paid by the telephone company for this endorsement. (smiling)

Again Baker brings up convenience. Typically a businessperson's thinking is geared to make buying decisions that are based on saving time and providing convenience. He also expects service. Baker casually drops another name.

BAKER: You know something, Bill, the typical person today is surprised when he gets good service. (a brief pause) That's too bad, because it should be the other way around. When it comes to servicing the customer, my philosophy is to give so much service that people feel guilty even *thinking* about doing business with someone else. Do you agree with me on this score, Bill?

Baker now begins to emphasize service—perhaps the number one difference that separates run-of-the-mill companies from great companies. Every businessperson appreciates good service, and again, Baker's question, "Do you agree with me on this score?" can be answered only affirmatively. Baker is trying to get Silver to agree with him again and again.

SILVER: Absolutely, Michael. I'm a real stickler about good service. And, you know, it just doesn't exist anymore. You go to the store and it's self-service—no clerks to wait on you. It's the same at the gas pumps. Or try to get a serviceman to repair your furnace. . . .

Again, Baker observes an important feature to stress: *good service*. However, Silver appears to be going off on a tangent, so Baker steps in and nips it in the bud.

BAKER: Speaking about service, we have an unbelievable maintenance program, Bill. (his rate of speech is increased) If you ever get a tear, a burn, or even if a button pops off, all you have to do is call me, and I'll pick up your suit and have it repaired for you. Now how many times have you had a rip in a perfectly good suit, but it's so darn inconvenient to take it to the tailor that you just let it hang in your closet for months at a time?

Since service is important to Silver, Baker emphasizes his unusual maintenance program, and hammers away at providing convenience.

SILVER: Yes, I know what you mean. I have a favorite navy blue suit at home that I don't wear because I lost some weight since I bought it a few years ago, and it needs to be taken in.

Baker makes a mental note that the prospect has a navy blue suit in poor condition.

BAKER: Now, if you had one of our suits, all you'd have to do is give me a call, and I'd come to your office, take your measurements, have it altered, and deliver it. Or, better yet, if your weight hadn't changed since your last suit with us, there'd be no need to take new measurements.

Here Baker vividly explains how his service program would work specifically for the prospect.

SILVER: That's terrific. I really appreciate that kind of service.

Silver's reaction is now positive, and Baker senses that he is winning his prospect over. He notices that Silver is now completely relaxed and, for the first time, actually *enthusiastic*.

BAKER: Well, I'm not going to keep it a secret, Bill. I want your business. And, I'll give you so much service that once you start doing business with me, you'll never consider another source. I'm not interested in doing business with you on a one-time basis—I'm in this for the long haul, and I plan to work with you for many, many years.

Baker continues to emphasize good service, and he lets the prospect know in no uncertain terms that *he wants his business*. Never be shy about letting someone know you want his business! And never hesitate to ask for it.

SILVER: I like what you're saying, Michael.

BAKER: Another thing, Bill, I'm a clothing expert. My specialty is catering to a very elite clientele who are extremely particular about their wardrobes. And in order to properly serve them, it's necessary for me to know my business backward and forward—which I do. I really do my homework, and I keep up to date on everything that happens in men's fashions. As you know, we live in a time where we must rely on consultants for just about everything— for taxes, legal services, decorating—you name it, and there's a consultant out there ready and eager to serve you. With all the information we're required to digest in today's hectic world, it's become very necessary to surround ourselves with experts to advise us. I'm sure that you have your share of consultants advising you. . . .

Here Baker toots his horn by letting Silver know that he's an expert in his field. He also emphasizes the importance of dealing with consultants in today's fast-moving world—which he knows a man like Silver must do on a regular basis.

SILVER: **Yeah, I'm up to here in consultants.** (raising his hand to his forehead) **But what can you do? Go on, I'm with you, Michael.**

The prospect continues to agree with Baker—a positive sign.

BAKER: **For instance, a certain suit might look good on a mannequin, but it doesn't look good on Bill Silver. I'm sure that you've bought a suit at one time or another, and while you liked it at the time of the purchase, you wore it once or twice and then let it just sit in your closet. . . .**

Baker brings up a common problem and creates a mental picture of it.

SILVER: **Yeah, I know what you mean.** (shaking his head) **I own several suits that I almost never wear.**

BAKER: **A major advantage of doing business with me is that I'm going to give you good, intelligent advice so you'll get the most wear out of every suit you buy, so you get your money's worth out of everything you own. I'll consult with you on the best colors for *you*, the best patterns for *you*, and the best styles that a man in your position should wear. The real value, Bill, will be that you'll feel very comfortable—and, most important, the upshot is that you'll feel confident about your appearance. Does this make sense to you?** (nodding his head)

He demonstrates how his consulting will benefit the prospect. Again he asks a question that anticipates a yes answer. (Note that it's hard for a person to say no when the other person is nodding yes.)

SILVER: **Yes, a lot of sense.** (nodding his head in agreement)

BAKER: **Now, I must point out that you may like a particular suit, and I won't think it's right for you. If this happens, I'm going to let you know it. Of course, you have the final word. But, if I strongly object, I won't keep it a secret. I'd rather not sell you a suit than have you make a poor decision. After all, my reputation is on the line, so I have a personal interest in what you buy from me. It's very important to me that you look terrific in a Winchester suit. Do you have any objection to my being very blunt and letting you know exactly how I feel?**

His candor takes Silver by surprise, but the prospect admires Baker's sincerity and conviction. This is also good reverse selling ("I'd rather not sell you a suit . . ."). Baker is also *assuming the sale* when he states that it's important to him for Silver to look terrific in a Winchester suit (Silver must buy one in order to look good in one!).

SILVER: **You're the expert. Say, Michael, when are you going to let me see what's in that briefcase?** (looking at his watch to indicate he's short of time)

By confirming that Baker is the expert, the prospect is acknowledging his acceptance. And, although Baker plans to show many samples of his merchandise to Silver, he isn't quite ready. Although the prospect wishes to see some swatches, Baker controls the sale by instead beginning his fact-finding mission (a series of questions that enables him to find out what the prospect's needs are). After all, how else will he know what to sell him!

BAKER: **Fine, I'll be happy to show you the finest selections of fabrics and patterns you've ever seen.** (he reaches for his briefcase as if to open it, but continues talking) **But, in order for me to give you the best possible service, first I'm going to have to find out more about you. Now there are a few questions I must ask you that I need for my files.** (brief pause) **Bill, I notice that you're wearing a lightweight suit. In fact, that looks like about an eight-and-a-half-ounce weight.** (as he talks, he takes out a memo pad and pencil) **Do you prefer lightweight fabrics year round, or do you only wear them on pleasant spring days like today and through the early fall?**

Keeping control of the interview, Baker begins his fact-finding mission. It's important to note that he didn't *ask* for the prospect's permission to question him. Instead, he assumed that it would be all right and simply started with a question. His first question was one that required some thought, rather than an easy inquiry that can be answered with an unconscious response. For this reason, it's recommended to ask a lead question that makes the prospect think of an answer—one that occupies his thought process. For example, if a simple question were asked, "What's your full name?" the prospect could answer rapidly and, while the salesperson was writing down the name, say, "Hey, what's going on? Why are you writing that down?"

SILVER: **Since I spend the vast majority of my time indoors, I don't wear heavy fabrics. I wear this weight practically all year. However, I**

have a couple of heavier weight that I wear on very cold days.

Giving a slight nod to acknowledge Silver's comments, Baker listens attentively, writing notes on a legal-size memo pad. Baker is well aware of the importance of *listening* to the prospect after asking a question. Not only does he encourage the prospect to participate in the conversation, but he continually invites him to express his thoughts.

BAKER: **We have many different wool fabrics. We have eighteen-ounce down to six-ounce wools. I'm wearing an eight-and-a-half-ounce suit.** (he holds out his sleeve so that the prospect can feel it) **I, too, personally wear this weight throughout the year. We also have some very fine worsted wools as well as fine blended wools. I'll show you some great fabrics in just a minute. Do you travel very much?**

Again, Baker points out that he has a large selection to satisfy the prospect. He also informs the prospect that he believes in his product—he's wearing it! He knows Silver is eager to see something he can look at and touch, but Baker continues to question him.

SILVER: **All the time. In fact, I'll be leaving for L.A. this afternoon. Tell me, do your wools wrinkle?**

BAKER: **All of our suits wrinkle. We don't make double-knits.** (he laughs)

Instead of denying that the suits wrinkle, he says that all of his suits do.

BAKER: **Some of our blends will hold a crease a little better than the wools. However, we also have wools with reverse twist weaving. At the risk** of getting too technical, they've cleared the yarn from two directions, providing it with a good diagonal give. This makes the garment wrinkle resistant. But, on one of our hot, humid summer days, nothing is sacred. (said with a smile) A natural fiber like wool is richer and more luxurious than a man-made fiber. While the polyesters hold a good crease and are wrinkle resistant, they won't absorb moisture like one-hundred-percent wool.

Although Baker makes it clear that he knows the clothing business, he doesn't confuse the prospect with a highly technical answer.

BAKER: Let me ask you some brief questions about your wardrobe now before I show you some swatches. (without waiting for a reply, he continues, with notepad in front of him, always with pen in hand) Do you usually select your clothing or does somebody do it for you?

SILVER: My wife, Ann, usually shops with me—but she lets me make the decision. (laughs)

BAKER: One of the nice things about my work, Bill, is that I deal with successful people who have the self-confidence to make decisions. Selecting a wardrobe is a minor decision in comparison to the major ones they make every day. (he raises his voice) I like dealing with men like you who have the ability to act—and don't procrastinate. Fortunately, I don't deal with Mr. Milquetoasts. That would bother me.

With this statement, Baker flatters the prospect, and lets Silver know that he will be disappointed in him if he can't make a buying decision later on—when it's time to close the sale. Baker's strategy is to let

Silver know that successful people aren't procrastinators and that they have the authority to make decisions on their own. Baker is setting the stage for the close—it will hurt the prospect's ego to appear as a Mr. Milquetoast.

BAKER: **Is there any particular line of clothing you prefer?**

Baker asks this question to give him a better idea of what quality clothes and price range Silver presently buys.

SILVER: **Many of my suits have the Meyer Brothers private label, but I also like Cambridge suits.**

BAKER: **Yes, Cambridge does a nice job with their clothes. (pause) Tell me, Bill, what condition is your present wardrobe in?**

After complimenting the competition, Baker follows through with another question.

SILVER: **I'm not sure I know exactly what you're getting at.**

BAKER: **Well, many busy people like yourself simply don't have the time or the inclination to shop, so they tend to neglect their wardrobes. Consequently, many of their suits are several years old, and, well, have a lot of mileage, or just aren't in style today.**

A statement of this nature must be tactfully made, without insulting the prospect.

SILVER: **I'd have to say my wardrobe is just so-so.**

BAKER: Is there anything in particular you feel should be added to your wardrobe?

Baker begins to probe.

SILVER: Mmm, nothing comes to mind. (thinking)

At this point, Baker remains silent, and several moments pass. Only when he feels that Silver has nothing to say does Baker continue.

BAKER: A navy blue suit is the most basic color for a businessperson of your stature, Bill. How many do you presently own?

Since Silver doesn't volunteer details, Baker continues to probe, becoming more specific. He will ask questions on a suit-by-suit basis, color by color. This is the first of a series of questions that Baker will ask to determine the prospect's needs.

SILVER: Well, that navy blue suit I mentioned before.

BAKER: The one in the closet that needs some alterations. How long have you had that suit, Bill?

SILVER: Oh, it's a good six years old.

BAKER: When was the last time you wore it?

SILVER: Mmm, let's see. (thinking) About two years ago.

Baker listens and remains silent. Finally, Silver speaks.

SILVER: I'm wondering if it could be altered. (pause) Or if it's even worth it. I guess it's somewhat dated by now.

BAKER: What do you mean "dated"?

He waits for a reply, believing that it's good for the prospect to articulate his discontent. Silver doesn't immediately volunteer information, but Baker waits him out until he finally replies.

SILVER: Well, the lapels are probably too wide, and it's slightly baggy on me. My wife keeps telling me to give it to charity, but you know, it's like parting with an old friend.

It isn't necessary to comment—Baker simply looks at Silver and gives a faint smile, as if to say, "You said it, I didn't." Remaining silent, Baker jots some notes on his memo pad that Silver needs a navy blue suit—and how fond he was of his old one.

BAKER: (breaking the silence) Okay, Bill, how about your grays? How many solid gray suits do you presently own?

SILVER: In solids? (thinking) Let's see, I used to have a dark gray flannel that I enjoyed wearing. But it's a little too heavy for me. I'm too warm in it so I hardly ever wear it. Maybe only once or twice a year—on very cold days.

BAKER: (continuing to take notes) One gray, hardly ever wears. (thinking out loud as he writes) Boy, do I have a classy banker's gray for you. (pause) How about your solid browns?

He continues to record Silver's remarks and asks more questions.

SILVER: I don't have any dark browns, but I do have a light summer khaki one that I enjoy wearing. Of course, it's very casual and I only knock around in it.

BAKER: That's fine. That's what it's for. What condition is it in?

SILVER: Oh, I bought it last spring. It's in good shape.

BAKER: Okay, khaki in good shape. (still thinking out loud as he writes) Let's discuss only your pinstripes now. What color pins do you have?

SILVER: I have several pins. Let's see, I have two dark blues. They look similar but one has a slightly wider stripe than this one that I'm wearing. And I have two grays. A light gray and a dark gray. Mmm, I guess that's about it. I have a couple of more older pinstripe suits too, but not worth mentioning because I don't wear them. They're in pretty bad shape.

BAKER: I don't need to know about the ones you never wear. But, the other dark blue . . . what condition is it in?

SILVER: This one is new. I've had it about a year, but the wide stripe is getting up there.

BAKER: How long have you had it?

SILVER: It's about seven years old.

BAKER: (continuing to take down notes as he talks) How often do you wear it?

SILVER: Actually, not much. I'll put it on only when I have nothing special going on that day.

BAKER: Why?

SILVER: I never really liked it that much. It was Ann's idea more than mine.

BAKER: **And this one?** (pointing to the suit Silver is wearing)

SILVER: **I wear it too much. Isn't it a beauty?** (his eyes light up, indicating his strong feelings)

BAKER: **Yes, I like it. Is this the suit you wear to your most important business functions?**

SILVER: **Yes. Board meetings and so on. I have an important dinner meeting in Los Angeles tonight, and I won't have time to change clothes.**

Baker makes a mental note on Silver's comment about how he chooses to wear his favorite suit for important occasions.

BAKER: (writing and talking) **Now the grays. First, the light gray. Describe it.**

SILVER: **A thin stripe, and it's more of a summer weight.**

BAKER: **Is it in good shape? How old is it?**

SILVER: **It's in good shape. About two years old.**

BAKER: **And the other gray?**

SILVER: **It's a dark gray and also has a faint whitish-blue stripe. It's strictly a business suit. It's about three years old and in good shape.**

BAKER: (still writing) **Okay, how about your plaids?**

SILVER: **I have a dark blue plaid, and a dark brown plaid. They're both a little heavy, so I don't wear them this time of year. They're four or five years old, and a little baggy. But I do wear them on occasion.**

By this time, Silver knows what questions to antici-
pate and volunteers the answers. This is viewed as a
good sign.

BAKER: **Do you ever wear sport jackets to work?**

SILVER: **No, but I wear them socially when the dress is
casual. Do you sell sport jackets too?**

BAKER: **Yes, we make wonderful sport jackets. But
let's concentrate on your suits now.** (reviewing
his notes) **Bill, which of your suits have vests?**

Not wanting to confuse the prospect, Baker decides
to focus strictly on making a suit sale. Once Silver
has become his client, Baker will seek his sports-coat
business. He maintains the philosophy, "If you chase
two rabbits, you don't catch either one." So, rather
than discussing sport jackets, he gets back on the
track by asking the question, "Which of your suits
have vests?"

SILVER: (thinking) **All four of my pinstripes and the
brown plaid.**

BAKER: **I notice you don't have your vest on today. Do
you wear the vests frequently?**

SILVER: **I used to, but recently I haven't. It seems as
though vests aren't quite as popular. I don't
see them around as much anymore. Are you
selling many suits with vests?**

BAKER: **Some men wear them all the time, but your
observation is correct—I'm not selling as many
vests as a few years ago.**

SILVER: **How do you personally feel about vests?**

BAKER: I like them, but I don't wear a vest every day. For instance, I have a vest for this suit, but I'm not wearing it today. When I do wear a vest, it gives a different look to this suit and makes me feel as though I'm wearing another outfit. From this viewpoint, a vest is worth the additional money. Secondly, I personally feel very businesslike when I wear the vest. For instance, I'd feel more confident in a vested suit if I were applying for a loan with my banker.

Not one to shy away from expressing his personal opinion, Baker explains his feelings about vested suits.

SILVER: How much are your vests?

BAKER: They run between one hundred and one fifty.

SILVER: That's a lot of money for just a vest, isn't it?

BAKER: It appears to be, but actually, Bill, there's a tremendous amount of material that goes into cutting a vest. And it's a time-consuming tailoring job.

First, Baker agrees with the prospect, and then he justifies the cost. He doesn't avoid discussing the price when asked.

BAKER: Okay, now, Bill, (carefully looking over his notes) is there any other suit you haven't mentioned?

He waits for Silver to reply. Silver is slow to give a reply, but Baker remains silent. He knows that a long pause can be effective in a sales presentation—at the right moment. He waits and waits until Silver responds.

SILVER: Mmm, I think that's it. (thinking) Oh, I forgot about my light gray suit. It's a medium-weight suit that I wear all year long—except on very hot days.

BAKER: It sounds like it's probably a ten-ounce weight, just a little heavier than my suit. Is it a solid color?

SILVER: Yes. And looks like a gray flannel suit except it's a Dacron and wool blend. (still thinking) Oh yes, I have another gray suit. It's a gray herringbone that I only wear in cold weather. I hardly wear it because it's too heavy and makes me perspire. And I have two seersuckers, a light gray and a light blue—but I rarely wear them in the office except when the temperature hits the high nineties.

BAKER: (writing down the information) Okay, is that it?

SILVER: I'm pretty sure I didn't leave anything out.

BAKER: Well, perhaps something else will come to mind while I'm showing you these swatches. (while he talks, he opens his briefcase and takes out some loose swatches that are bound together at the top) Now if you think of anything that you left out, please let me know. I need to know your complete wardrobe in order to provide you with the best possible service.

During Baker's fact-finding session, he has greatly impressed the prospect with the fact that he has genuine interest in his welfare. He has demonstrated his sincerity by professionally and thoroughly cross-examining Silver—*taking the time to really find out about his needs* instead of rushing through the presentation in order to make a quick sale. Throughout the entire fact-finding session, Baker's eyes are fixed on the prospect's eyes, allowing nothing to distract him.

Up to this point in the presentation, nothing tangible has been given to the prospect that he could see or touch. It's now time for Baker to show his merchandise.

BAKER: **Bill, other than a tuxedo, there's nothing more elegant in a man's wardrobe than a dark blue suit. Blue happens to be very flattering to you because it goes well with your eyes and coloring. A solid navy blue is also considered to be our "power" suit—at least that's what the psychologists tell us. Blue represents strength and vitality. (pause) Now, these are all eight-and-a-half-ounce wools.**

As Baker puts five swatches on the table, he continues to talk. Baker's choice of the color blue is based on Silver's comment about his favorite old blue suit hanging in the closet. Although he has a large selection in his briefcase, he doesn't want to overwhelm and confuse the prospect by showing too much. A selection of five is enough for now.

SILVER: (after touching and studying the swatches while Baker remains silent) **This is a perfect weight. Is this the same as the suit you're wearing, Michael?**

BAKER: **Exactly.**

He remains silent and lets the prospect think.

SILVER: **I like these two best. Which one do you recommend, Michael?**

BAKER: **They're both beauties, but I like the darker one best. It's perfect with your coloring.**

Since he's asked, Baker gives his honest opinion.

SILVER: **I'm afraid I'm not very good at this. (pause) I'm having a difficult time visualizing how this swatch will look in a suit.**

BAKER: **Yes, I know what you mean. Many of my clients have said the same thing when I first called on them. Ed Westhaven, TBR's chairman, had the darnedest time when I first started working with him. But now Ed says he'd never buy another suit any other way. In fact, I had the same problem myself.**

Instead of denying the problem, Baker expresses his understanding. He also takes the opportunity to drop another impressive client's name. But he doesn't make a major issue of it.

SILVER: **Ed buys from you too? I like the way he dresses.**

BAKER: **Yes, and I'm sure you can visualize him in a dark blue suit like this.**

He paints a picture for Silver—in living color.

BAKER: **Here, let's take this swatch and place it on your sleeve. (he drapes the swatch over Silver's arm) Now look at it. Isn't that elegant? (nodding his head)**

He brings the prospect into the act by letting him participate.

SILVER: (pensively) **I like it, and I suppose I could use a new blue suit. . . .**

BAKER: **Let me put these solid blues aside for now.** (he pauses briefly and picks up his pen) **Bill, I need that number on the swatch. Read it to me, would you please?** (pointing to it in front of Silver)

Although Baker could have read the number himself, he wants to keep the prospect occupied and to let him participate in the sale. He's also assuming the sale. When Silver consents to give the swatch number, it's as if he is saying, "Yes, I will buy the suit."

SILVER: **You mean this one? S291M216.**

BAKER: **Yes, that's it. Thank you.** (he writes it on his pad) **Now, Bill, I also want to show you what I think is a classic suit that every man in your position must have in his wardrobe.**

Baker has the option of either writing up the order for one suit or continuing his presentation and selling an additional suit(s). He is feeling confident and opts to sell at least one more suit. After all, he has a receptive prospect who has both the need and the wherewithal. Under these circumstances, believing that the odds are in his favor, Baker places five more swatches in front of Silver.

BAKER: **These charcoal grays are magnificent, aren't they?** (he nods his head and waits for Silver to agree) **This fabric is also eight-and-a-half-ounce wool.**

SILVER: **This one looks a lot like my old gray flannel suit that I don't wear because it's not comfortable.**

BAKER: Yes, and you said how much you loved your gray flannel. I agree, it's a very impressive-looking suit. And you're right—a lot of men are uncomfortable wearing flannel. However, this charcoal gray wool has the same look, and it feels great. (pause) **Feel that fabric. See how light it is?**

Knowing how much Silver enjoyed the look of his gray flannel, Baker whets his prospect's appetite by showing him similar colors in a lightweight fabric. Silver carefully studies the five fabrics.

SILVER: I think this one is nice. (pause) **Which one do you like for me, Michael?**

BAKER: They're all nice, but since you asked me for my opinion, I recommend this one. (he hands it to Silver to examine) **Of course, you can't go wrong with any of them.**

Again Baker states his opinion when asked for one.

SILVER: (examining it) Yes, I like this. But I'm still having a difficult time visualizing myself in the actual suit. (pause) **When I buy a suit in a store, I try it on to see how it will look.**

BAKER: That's why I'm here, Bill. Remember, I'm your consultant and *I'm an expert in this business.* I *know* what you'll look good in, and I won't let you buy anything unless I'm one hundred percent sure about it.

Seeing that the prospect is unsure, Baker again confirms that he is an expert—and the prospect should trust his judgment.

BAKER: This shade is appropriately called "banker's gray." I'm sure you've probably heard people refer to it, haven't you?

SILVER: (studying the swatch) Yes.

BAKER: Gray is very distinguished and understated. It's perfect for you.

A final statement to fully convince Silver . . .

BAKER: Read its number to me, will you please?

Assuming the sale, he again asks for the swatch number, and as Silver gives it to him, he writes it down. After he puts aside the gray swatches, Baker decides to sell a third suit and pulls out five more swatches.

BAKER: Bill, I want you to look at these brown pin-stripes. Now, a brown pinstripe would be a nice addition to your present wardrobe. And feel this fabric. This is a ten-ounce worsted wool. It's closely woven from a smooth, well-twisted yarn. Interesting, isn't it?

After handing them to Silver, he remains silent.

SILVER: (shaking his head) No, they don't do anything for me.

BAKER: Okay, let's put them away then. (he places them back in his briefcase) I want to show you one more thing—some gray plaids that I think are very nice.

Reading Silver's initial reaction to the brown pin-stripes, Baker doesn't push it. Instead, he makes an attempt to sell something else, still feeling confident that an even larger order is possible.

SILVER: I'm not wild about plaids, and I already have a blue and a brown that my wife picked out.

BAKER: Bill, wait until you see these before you pass judgment. These have a subdued pattern that's very different from your ordinary plaids. (he places five swatches on the table) You have to look closely to actually see the plaid. Aren't these beautiful?

Baker tests the water to see what kind of a reaction Silver has to the gray plaid swatches. He remains silent, waiting for the prospect to speak first. While Silver studies the swatches, Baker keeps busy by reading over his notes, marking down a few thoughts.

SILVER: (handling one plaid in particular) This is interesting.

BAKER: Stand back and look at it. I want you to see how subtle that plaid is.

Again, he gives Silver a slight order, controlling the sale, and getting him into the act.

SILVER: Yes, I see what you mean. This is beautiful. How do you feel about this one?

BAKER: I agree with you. That's my favorite, and it's perfect for you.

After agreeing with Silver, Baker again asks for the swatch number, once more assuming the sale. Again, Silver gives him the number, and Baker thanks him.

Baker has decided not to try to sell another suit. Based on past experience, he senses Silver's limit is three new suits on the first call. Baker carefully studies his notes, then reaches into his briefcase for a form.

BAKER: Okay, Bill, stand up. I want to take your measurements. You wear a forty-four long and have a thirty-five inch waist. . . .

Notice that he doesn't say, "Is it okay if I take your measurements?" Instead, Baker assumes he may, by taking out his tape, and begins to measure the prospect as if he had consented. Had he asked for permission to take his measurements, Silver might have said, "Now wait a minute. I'm not ready to buy."

BAKER: How tall are you, Bill?

SILVER: Six-two. (pausing) Hey, I didn't say I was buying today. Aren't you putting the cart before the horse?

BAKER: I need your measurements, Bill. What's your present weight?

Rather than making an issue out of the statement, "I didn't say I was buying today," Baker wisely passes over it and continues to ask questions. If Baker had asked, "Why won't you buy a suit today?" Silver could state his objection, and perhaps, in order to save face, feel obligated to stick to it. It's poor selling to back a prospect into a corner where he is forced to take a stand and must defend his position.

SILVER: Two hundred eight pounds.

BAKER: Does your weight fluctuate very much?

SILVER: Only a few pounds a year, particularly around the Christmas holidays.

BAKER: (measuring Silver) Okay, now your left leg inseam measures thirty-six, and your right leg inseam is thirty-six and seven-eighths. Your hips are thirty-eight. Your left arm is thirty-five and a half and your right arm is thirty-six and a quarter. What size dress shirts do you normally wear?

SILVER: My neck is seventeen and the sleeves are thirty-five and a half.

BAKER: (measuring his neck) My measurements show your neck is seventeen and a quarter. Keep in mind that custom-made clothing is more exact than off-the-rack clothing.

As Silver stands erect, Baker thoroughly measures him, making comments and writing down measurements at the same time. He keeps giving the prospect little orders such as, "Face this way." "Turn that way." "Let your arm down." "Relax it." "Inhale." "Exhale." By getting the prospect conditioned to take small, unassuming orders, it will later be easy for Baker to give the order, "Make out your check" when he closes the sale.

By giving extreme attention to detail, Baker demonstrates professionalism and his desire to serve his customer. Throughout the measurement-taking process, he asks, "Do you like your sleeve this length or this length?" "Do you like a slight break in the pants?" "Do you like your waist with just a little slack such as this, or is this more comfortable to you?" After several minutes of measuring, questioning, and writing down information, Baker finishes.

BAKER: Bill, I'm sure you can appreciate that these measurements must be taken in order to make a tailor-made suit with an exact fit. Now that we have them, we'll keep them on file, and unless your weight changes drastically, it won't be necessary to go through all of this again.

After the measurements are taken, Baker explains that he won't have to take the measurements when Silver buys in the future—again assuming the sale, now and later!

SILVER: (sighing) That's a relief!

BAKER: Now, I want to make sure the suit is made exactly the way you want it. Again, this is a major advantage when we start from scratch versus buying what's hanging there on the rack.

As he asks a series of questions, he takes out a six-page brochure with drawings of various suits and points to different models so that the prospect can understand each question.

BAKER: Do you want three buttons or two? Which buttons do you like best? Which type flaps on the pockets do you like? Which of these cuts do you like for the jacket? Which of these two vents do you like? I recommend the hook vent. Which stitching do you prefer? Which pocket do you like on the pants? With or without belt loops? Which belt loops? Do you like the pleats or nonpleats? Cuffs or no cuffs? What length cuffs?

Baker allows the prospect enough time to answer each question. He demonstrates patience, never rushing the prospect. Silver recognizes Baker's genuine desire to serve him. When Baker is asked, he makes a recommendation—as he does when Silver shows hesitation and can't make up his mind. As the prospect answers each question, he is committing himself to buy. It's assumed that he is buying—why else would he volunteer this kind of information!

When the final question is asked, Baker carefully studies the application. He then places the three swatches representing the navy blue, charcoal gray, and gray plaid suits in front of him.

BAKER: **These are magnificent, Bill. I'm looking forward to seeing you in them. You'll look great in all three.** (he writes a brief description and swatch number on the application) **Now the two solids are four hundred seventy-five dollars each, and the gray plaid is five hundred twenty-five. The vests for each suit run one hundred twenty dollars even. I'll put down a vest for each suit.**

Still assuming the sale, Baker writes the three suits on the order form and nonchalantly quotes the price of each suit. Rather than asking, "Do you want a vest?" he says, "I'll put down a vest for each suit." Note that he says this with the assumption that Silver wants three vests.

SILVER: **Four seventy-five? Five twenty-five?** (surprised, he repeats the prices) **I thought you said your suits were priced at three hundred seventy-five.**

BAKER: **Our blends start at three seventy-five. But, four seventy-five and five twenty-five for a completed tailored *wool* suit is an outstanding value. Which suits do you want with vests?**

Rather than hemming and hawing when the prospect resists the price, Baker confidently states that his prices represent value. He then closes again by asking *which* vests the prospect wants. This is what is known as a minor-major closing technique. Silver is asked to make a minor buying decision to *buy a vest(s) instead of an entire suit*.

SILVER: I'm going to pass on the vests, and I don't want all three suits. I'd like to try one of them out first.

BAKER: (softly) May I make a suggestion, Bill?

Rarely does anyone object to someone making a suggestion.

SILVER: Yes. What?

BAKER: Let's get the navy blue and the charcoal gray. You desperately need a navy blue. Every well-dressed executive must have a navy blue suit in his wardrobe. And I know you're going to love the gray. (pause) I also recommend getting the vest with the charcoal gray.

Notice that he says, "Let's (*Let us*—a joint decision) get the navy blue and the charcoal gray." A joint decision is easier to make than a unilateral one because if it turns out to be wrong, the blame can be shared—or put on the other party! Baker then reinforces Silver's need for a blue suit and reminds him how much he'll love the gray.

SILVER: (thinking) I'd like to sleep on it. I'll let you know when I return from L.A.

BAKER: Bill, you have more important things to think about on your trip than this. I recommend that we get your order in immediately. The home office has informed me that our inventory on blues and grays in the wool fabrics is running low. If a shortage occurs, it could take anywhere from three to six months before the company gets delivery from the mills. Now, I know that you're not going to want to wait for ninety to one hundred eighty days, so let's get the order in immediately.

First Baker minimizes the importance of the buying decision, then he creates a sense of urgency—giving a reason why the prospect should *act now*. In this case, the urgency is a lack of availability if the buying decision is delayed.

SILVER: How long does it take for delivery, Michael?

By asking this question, Baker assumes that Silver has accepted his recommendation.

BAKER: Approximately six weeks. Now I'll call you as soon as your order is ready and set up an appointment to come back for a fitting. If, for any reason, something isn't just right, I'll take it back for alterations.

He assumes the sale by explaining the delivery procedure. Without hesitation, he begins to write in the figures and add up the sale.

BAKER: Let's see now, that comes to ten seventy [$1,070]. And with the six percent sales tax of sixty-four twenty [$64.20], a total of eleven thirty-four twenty [$1,134.20]. Do you want to pay this by credit card or check?

Baker isn't shy about asking for money. However, notice that he says *ten seventy* rather than *one thousand and seventy dollars* because ten seventy sounds like less money. Using a minor-major close, he gives the prospect an easy decision to make: a choice to pay by credit card or a check. In a minor-major close, the prospect is asked to make easy minor decisions rather than a more difficult major decision.

SILVER: I'll pay by check.

BAKER: Make your check payable to Winchester Associates. I'll make out your receipt.

Assuming the sale (and keeping control), Baker gives a small order—"Make your check payable to Winchester Associates."

SILVER: Do I have to pay for it all now?

BAKER: You may pay half now and the balance on delivery, or the full amount now. Which do you prefer?

The first time, he asked for the entire amount, but he now offers him a choice of two. Had Silver not asked, "Do I have to pay it all now?" Baker would not have mentioned that there was an option to pay only half. Again, he assumes that the prospect will pay either half or in full. Once more, a minor decision is required: to pay either half or the full price now. Baker also prepares the prospect for what he must pay at the time of delivery.

SILVER: I'd rather not pay the full amount now. (pausing) And what happens if I don't like the finished suit?

This remark indicates that Silver has some reservations.

BAKER: I will personally deliver your suits to you, and if you're not completely satisfied, I'll make sure that the problem is corrected. That's one of the reasons I take the time to deliver our merchandise. Let's say, for example, Bill, the tailoring isn't a perfect fit—perhaps you put on a few pounds in the next few weeks and we have to let a little out in the waist. In that case, I'll retake your measurements and our tailor will make the necessary alterations. Now, as far as not wanting to pay the full amount today, that's fine. Make out your check in the amount of five sixty-seven ten [$567.10] to Winchester Associates.

Sensing that Silver has some doubt, Baker gives a detailed answer to his questions—and then, not being bashful about asking for money, he requests a half-payment deposit. He hands an invoice to the prospect and points to the dollar amount.

SILVER: But what if I don't like the looks of the suit? What if I'm not satisfied with how I look in it?

BAKER: How can you *not* know how you'll look in a navy blue and a charcoal gray suit? They'll look terrific on you. (pause) Look, Bill, you're a businessperson, so I know you understand that once we custom-make these suits to your exact measurements, they can *only* be worn by you. So, if you're not absolutely certain that you want them, this is the time to say so. (pause) But, let's not make a big deal out of this transaction. You're only buying two suits. We're talking about a small-potatoes decision for a man in your position.

Baker is straightforward with Silver and lets him know that his buying decision is irrevocable. Had he let him off the hook by insinuating that Silver could get his money back if he wasn't satisfied, at best it would have been an iffy sale. Baker's lighthearted comment about it not being a "big deal" breaks up an otherwise tense moment and relaxes the prospect.

SILVER: **Did you say I could pay half now?**

BAKER: **Yes. You can make out your check to Winchester Associates while I make out your receipt.**

He assumes the sale and instructs the prospect to make out his check.

At this point, Silver gets up to get a check from his desk. He writes it out and hands it to Baker.

BAKER: **Congratulations, Bill. You're going to love your new suits.**

Baker doesn't reach for the check but instead lets Silver place it on the table. He ignores the check, not wanting to appear overly eager to have the money. He continues talking, congratulating Silver, making him feel good about his decision. Baker then decides to do some prospecting before he leaves.

BAKER: **Before I leave, Bill, I'd like to ask you a favor.**

Most people are willing to do you a favor—all you have to do is *ask* them.

SILVER: **Sure. What's the favor?**

BAKER: **As you know, I do business with a very discriminating clientele. With this in mind, my success depends on personal recommendations from centers of influence—VIPs like yourself. Whom do you know that you'd like to recommend to me? Think of somebody like yourself,**

who would appreciate our high quality, outstanding values, and tremendous selections.
And—again somebody like yourself—who places
a high premium on his time.

Baker flatters Silver by referring to him as a center
of influence, briefly reiterates the main selling points
of his presentation (thereby solidifying the sale once
again), and, knowing that prospecting is the lifeblood
of his business, asks Silver for referrals.

SILVER: Gosh, you caught me off guard. (thinking) I
can't think of anyone. Let me think about it.

BAKER: Is there anyone here at National Manufacturing whom you'd recommend?

When asking for referrals, it's wise to make suggestions.

SILVER: (thinking) It's hard to say who would be in
the market.

BAKER: Anyone who appreciates fine clothes is in
the market. How about one of your senior
executives?

When Silver can't come up with any names, Baker
gets specific, giving him ideas for potential prospects.

SILVER: Our sales manager, Matthew Meyer, would
be good. And you should see Roger Benjamin,
our executive vice-president.

Baker writes down both names and continues to ask
for additional names.

BAKER: How about your comptroller?

He continues to pump Silver for names.

SILVER: Yes, that's Robert James.

BAKER: Who does your legal work?

Again, more suggestions—making it easy for Silver to think of leads.

SILVER: Stan Glick. He's tough on salesmen, but he loves fine suits.

BAKER: He's a pussycat. Stan has been buying suits from me for three years.

By mentioning that he sold to Glick, a *tough cookie*, who has a reputation for being a difficult person to sell, Baker has impressed Silver by letting him think: "If he could sell Glick, his merchandise must really be good."

SILVER: No kidding? You sell Glick?

BAKER: Yes sir. (pausing) How about the guys in your foursome?

Looking around the office, Baker spots a golf trophy on the credenza. As a matter of habit, Baker looks for clues in a prospect's office that provide hints of his interests. Similar clues might appear in photos, framed certificates, books, and so on. Baker continues to push for more names.

SILVER: Yes, Chuck Roth, who owns Roth Advertising, and Al Wein, who's a cardiologist. The fourth is a building contractor and could care less about how he dresses. (looking at his watch) Look, Michael, I'm running out of time. How about if I think of some more names and give them to you later?

BAKER: That would be wonderful, and I appreciate these names. Oh, one more thing. You wouldn't have any problem if I mentioned your name to these people, would you?

Always ask for permission to use somebody's name when getting referrals. With the technique that Baker uses when he asks, it's hard for anyone to refuse.

SILVER: No, go right ahead and tell them I sent you.

BAKER: Thank you very much. And thank you for your business. May this be the beginning of a lifetime friendship for us, Bill.

SILVER: It's been a real pleasure to meet you. Thank you, Michael.

PART III
AFTER THE
PRESENTATION

The After-the-Sale Letter

After the sale, Michael Baker sends the following letter to every new customer:

Dear Bill:

I enjoyed meeting you today, and again want you to know how much I appreciate your business. Congratulations on your good judgment and fine taste. I know you will get years of pleasure out of your new suits.

In approximately six weeks your suits will be ready, and at such time I will call you to set up an appointment for delivery. In the meantime, should you have any questions, please don't hesitate to call me.

May this be the beginning of a long friendship. I look forward to providing you with outstanding service regarding your clothing needs for many years.

Again, many thanks.

Sincerely,
Michael Baker

Every salesperson should routinely send a personal thank-you letter to all customers, preferably the same day of the sale. A handwritten, informal note is recommended, although a typewritten letter is acceptable.

Unfortunately, it's rare that a customer receives a thank-you letter from a salesperson. Chances are that you didn't receive one the last time you bought a car, a house, or a home computer. Yet, it's such a simple thing to do and creates so much goodwill.

A thank-you letter accomplishes the following:

1. *Demonstrates courtesy.* It's good etiquette to take the time and effort to let someone know that you appreciate his or her business (for this reason alone, all salespersons should send them to their customers).

2. *Establishes good rapport.* Each time you have contact with your customer, you're building the foundation for what you hope will be a long-term relationship. The letter is an inexpensive tool that helps create goodwill—it will cause him to think good thoughts about you.

3. *Reduces buyer's remorse.* Frequently, shortly after the sale, some people have a tendency to "cool off." In Silver's case, he may have second thoughts about spending $1,134.20 for two suits. He could even think, "Is Winchester Associates as good as Michael Baker claims? Did he really mean it when he talked about giving good service, or was he only giving lip service just to get the sale?" All too often the customer has good reason to complain, "Sure, a salesperson is always there to sell you, but where is he when you need him [service]?" Baker's letter confirms that he is conscientious and helps substantiate Silver's initial judgment—buying two suits was a good decision. The letter provides peace of mind, and *makes him feel good about his buying decision.*

Following Up
After the Sale

Every successful professional salesperson knows that once the sale is closed, it's just the beginning. While a two-suit order compensates Michael Baker very nicely for his time spent with Bill Silver, this initial sale represents only the first of many future orders—if he does his job properly. As Baker puts it, "I'm not in business for the one-time sale. My success is dependent upon repeat sales that result from giving tender loving care to my customers." In the long run, servicing the customer is what successful selling is all about.

As Baker told Silver, "My philosophy is to give so much service that people feel guilty even *thinking* about doing business with someone else." While Baker is well aware that he has a good product, he also knows that Winchester Associates doesn't have a monopoly on fine men's clothing. Nor, for that matter, does any other company! Good service is what separates truly great companies (and salespersons) from those that are run-of-the-mill. In today's highly competitive business world, good service is essential. Gone are the days when a fast-talking salesman's success could rely on a good gift of gab, a dirty joke, and a slap on the customer's back.

Servicing the customer is a continuous obligation of every salesperson. Considerable behind-the-scenes work must be done *after* the sale. For instance, an insurance agent might be required to schedule appointments for physical examinations for the applicant, contact attorneys and accountants, and follow up with the insurance company's underwriting department on unusual delays in the issuance of the policy. A real estate agent might help secure the mortgage, attain an abstract on the property, and serve as a liaison between the buyer and the seller until the title is transferred. Likewise, a computer salesperson's job just begins at the time of the close; the installation of a system is frequently as long as a year or more down the road. If the salesperson fails to perform after the sale, he or she will probably not be able to make future sales to that customer. Follow-up work is mandatory, either by the salesperson or by a capable assistant. Frequently, many top producers successfully delegate this work to another person.

Like many salespeople, Baker must complete a lot of paperwork to process his customer's order. During the sales presentation he meticulously jotted down notes on a memo pad, which must now be transferred to Winchester's standard order forms. Baker also makes up an individual file on every prospect and client. In his file on Silver he keeps records on such things as:

- his secretary's and receptionist's names;
- his spouse's name;
- his existing wardrobe;
- complete data on Winchester suits purchased (colors, styles, fabrics, etc.);
- customer's measurements;
- his birthdate (Baker routinely sends birthday cards and Christmas cards);
- his hobbies (golf, etc.);
- the best time(s) of day to call on him;
- referrals (with names, addresses, occupations, positions, remarks made about them by the customer, etc.), and so on.

Baker also records information on all contact he has with each client, including relevant discussions to refer to during future conversations. And since Baker is in the clothing business, he even jots down the suit he wears—to avoid wearing the same outfit on a later visit. Recently he purchased a home computer to store individual files on his many clients.

To avoid "down time," Baker does his paperwork during nonselling hours—evenings and weekends. Every order he takes is routinely mailed to Winchester the following morning. Often he must do his paperwork late at night, since much of his time is devoted to activities in civic and charitable organizations. "I believe in paying my dues to the community that provides me with my livelihood," he says, "not to mention the contacts I make with many of the town's leading business and professional people who are also actively involved in the community." How does he manage to put in long hours in the field and be active in the community? As he puts it, "If you want something done, ask a busy man to do it." Like all top sales leaders, he excels in good time management.

How to Manage Problems After the Sale

Sooner or later, every salesperson will encounter problems that necessitate making a "difficult" call—informing a new hard-to-sell customer that something has gone haywire with his order. The best way to handle these situations is *promptly* and *directly*, always getting right to the point. Don't procrastinate—make the call immediately. A few weeks have expired since his sales presentation to Bill Silver, and now Michael Baker must deal with such a problem. Winchester Associates has temporarily run out of the gray fabric for Silver's suit and has reordered more, causing a three-week delay on the suit. Additionally, the blue fabric won't be available for six months. Baker calls Silver to relay the bad news.

BAKER: Bill, we have a problem on your order. The demand for the dark gray fabric has been running so great that the company's inventory has been temporarily exhausted. Consequently, your suit will be delayed for three weeks.

SILVER: That's no big problem, Michael. I appreciate your calling.

BAKER: You're not going to believe it, but the company is also out of the blue fabric. This is unbelievable, Bill. This has never happened with two suits to the same client. I'm really sorry.

SILVER: Don't worry about it. You'll just bring the blue with the gray.

BAKER: Bill, I've got some bad news and some good news. What do you want to hear first, the bad news or the good news?

SILVER: What's the bad news?

BAKER: The bad news is that the mill is running behind and can't deliver the fabric to us for six months. But the good news is that I have another fabric that is almost identical. In fact, it's a magnificent wool with only a slightly different weave. It's the same weight and color, just a smidgen difference that you'd probably never notice. Now, the suit in this fabric runs five hundred and twenty-five dollars. . . .

SILVER: That's an extra fifty dollars. You call that good news?

BAKER: I talked to the company about it and they said you could have it for four seventy-five, the same price as the other blue fabric. If you'd like, I'll stop in your office sometime later this week and show it to you for your approval.

SILVER: Michael, if you like it, that's good enough for me. See you in a few weeks, and thanks for the call.

Baker handled a potentially serious problem perfectly. His call to Silver nipped in the bud a problem that, if left unattended, could have blown the sale. Instead, he created good will, presenting himself as both straightforward and conscientious. If everything goes smoothly, his next telephone conversation with Silver will take place when the order is ready for delivery. In the meantime, the beginning of a long-term salesperson/customer relationship is developing—and that's what professional selling is all about.

PART IV
COMMENTARY ON THE PERFECT SALES PRESENTATION

Note to the
Reader

The Perfect Sales Presentation is a composite of the best selling techniques and attributes of the five sales experts. In this section, Mary Kay Ash, Joe Gandolfo, Bettye Hardeman, Buck Rodgers, and Martin Shafiroff comment on Michael Baker's presentation. Here, each expresses his or her expertise and addresses the following ten items:

Doing Your Homework *Before* the Presentation
Getting Past the Gatekeeper on the Telephone
Creating Initial Interest
The Fact-Finding Session
Presenting the Product
Controlling the Sale
Assuming the Sale
Overcoming Objections
Closing the Sale
Servicing the Customer

Doing Your Homework *Before* the Sales Presentation

Obviously, from the way Baker has organized his prospect notecards, he has done his homework in advance. For this reason, he is able to use his time productively on the telephone during a forty-five-minute break that results from a canceled appointment. He has arranged his leads in a concentrated section of town to avoid spending "down time" in his car, driving long distances between calls.

Each of the five sales experts uses his or her time in a similar manner, always well aware of the value of time. Shafiroff feels that "every salesperson worth his or her salt is a good time manager." He states, "There are only so many minutes in each day, and just how well you make use of them is often what separates star sales performers from mediocre performers. Common sense dictates that if two salespersons have equal ability, and one gives twice as many presentations, he will produce at least twice as many sales. And when you consider the principle of synergy, his productivity may be far greater— resulting in three or four times as many sales. For this reason, every salesperson must carefully prepare his day in advance, making sure his prime selling time is used in front of the customer. With a broken appointment, Baker does what is the second most valuable use of his time [selling is number one]: he uses it to set up future appointments. Only during his 'off hours,' the time of the day [or night] when customers can't readily be contacted, should a salesperson be engaged in nonselling activities." Shafiroff believes that everything else is secondary to good time management and commends Baker for realizing the importance of contacting customers during his prime selling hours.

Joe Gandolfo states that during his working time, he does not engage in a single activity that isn't related to selling. "Every meal has a purpose," he explains. "Anyone I eat with is either a client or somebody who can help me to make money. Even when I eat alone, I'm either on the phone or reading business-related material. Every person I speak with during the day has something to do with my selling. There are 1,440 minutes in every 24-hour period, and I cherish every one of them during my work day." His thinking, like Shafiroff's, reflects the other three sales experts'; each is a master at getting the most mileage out of his or her time.

While Baker's preparation in product knowledge is not portrayed in this book, it is evident from his expertise about the clothing industry that he has spent many behind-the-scene hours doing his homework. "He demonstrates his product knowledge very well," comments Buck Rodgers, "in his ability to present his line so thoroughly and the manner in which he answers rebuttals. Every professional salesperson I've ever known does his or her homework in advance—and it doesn't take long before the customer realizes it. If you fail to prepare yourself before the call, you'll waste a lot of your customer's time, and you insult him.

"Selling is really no different from any other profession," Rodgers continues. "The surgeon who removes your gallbladder studied medicine, did his internship, and is properly licensed to practice his profession. You wouldn't expect him to walk into the operating room without having been properly prepared. As in any profession—medicine, law, accounting, architecture—

customers deserve the same treatment from the professional salesperson."

Rodgers explains how every IBM rep receives a full year's training of combined classroom and in-the-field selling, so that by the time he is face to face with a customer he's well prepared. And, at IBM, each marketing rep specializes according to industry. For example, one rep might call only on people in banking, another in retailing, and another in manufacturing. Each has been trained to understand the specific problems in a given industry.

"The days are long gone when someone walks down the street calling on every prospect in the block," Rodgers points out. "Specialization by industry allows a salesperson to speak the customer's language. It's a very solution-oriented approach to selling. Furthermore, nobody ever makes a call without doing some homework on the customer himself. For example, if an IBMer is assigned a particular account, he will spend some time reviewing which of our systems are presently being used by the customer. He'll also do some research on the company itself, perhaps by first reading the annual report and 10-K report. Of course, this kind of homework isn't required for Baker, because selling men's apparel has little to do with the operation of a business. It is important, however, for him to know the nature of a prospect's business, not only to talk intelligently about it to the prospect, but also to perceive what dress is appropriate in the work place, for attending conferences, and so on. I'm sure that Baker finds the dress code in some industries more formal than in others."

While selling computer systems may be considerably more complex than selling cosmetics, Mary Kay Ash stresses that each Mary Kay beauty consultant must also be thoroughly knowledgeable in her product line. "Our reps must be experts in both products and skin care techniques," she points out, "because they conduct skin-care classes. In this capacity, they play the role of instructors and their selling is actually a form of teaching. There's a great deal of behind-the-scenes preparation that they must do in order to come across as qualified consultants. This is particularly true in a group sales presentation. Nothing is potentially more embarrassing than to get up in front of a group of people and not know what you're talking about."

In the case of a product like real estate, selling multiple listed properties such as Bettye Hardeman does in Atlanta, every agent in town literally can sell the identical properties. For this reason, her real estate expertise and willingness to do her homework for every client in advance is her biggest edge. "I've got to keep up with the market at all times," she says. "I must know all the properties that become available, and I'm constantly reviewing the new-home sheets that come into my office. Before I take a prospect out to show a new home, I make it my business to inspect it in person whenever possible. On the rare occasions that I don't, I make sure I've spoken to the listing agent to know all of its important features."

Bettye Hardeman also stresses that today's real estate agent must be very knowledgeable about financing. "Knowing what kinds of loans are available for real estate is essential," she states. "And there are so many ways to finance a home today. The finance market is ever-changing, and unless I keep abreast of it, I can't properly serve my client."

Since the clothing and cosmetics industries are both fashion oriented, Ash is quick to recognize Baker's immaculate appearance. "When one of our reps walks through the door, it's vital that she look like a beauty consultant. Her hair and makeup are impeccable, her nails are well manicured, her dress is in vogue, her hose don't have any runs, her shoes are spotless—in short, her appearance is attractive and professional. Because if she's going to sell beauty, her objective is to get her prospect[s] to want to look like her. There's no way somebody is going to take advice from a beauty consultant who looks sloppy and slovenly. Baker also recognizes that his appearance is essential. His ability to consult his customers on proper dress would be greatly diminished if he wasn't dressed properly. They'd think, 'What can he tell me about how to dress?'

"Equally important, a salesperson must be prepared mentally," Ash adds. "This means leaving your troubles at home when you approach a prospect. I don't care if the water heater just broke, your children have smallpox, and your spouse just lost his job. You must never take your problems to your customer. You must turn off your problems and approach every sale with enthusiasm. No matter how many personal problems I might have had, whenever I walked through a prospect's door, I put on a happy face, and nobody ever suspected that behind my big smile I sometimes had all sorts of troubles."

Rodgers concurs that a salesperson must be mentally prepared before he or she makes sales calls. "Selling is a piece of cake when prospects are out there, waiting for you with open arms," he states. "But, no matter what you sell, it's not like that in the real world. Regardless of what you sell, you're bound to get rejection if you make enough calls. It's just part of the selling game. And I have yet to meet anyone who likes rejection. When a salesperson gets shot out of the saddle several times in a row, he must be strong enough to accept it, always believing in his ability, his company, and his product. This kind of confidence comes from being properly prepared—knowing that if he keeps making enough calls, he'll succeed. I've never met a person who achieved lasting success in sales who didn't think this way."

Getting Past the Gatekeeper on the Telephone

Understandably, all five sales experts place a high value on their time. Unanimously, they agree that the telephone is an excellent time-saving tool to set up appointments for sales presentations. However, there is one major hurdle that you must overcome in order to make contact with your prospect: the gatekeeper. This is the individual whose job is to screen telephone calls for the boss. The gatekeeper is usually an assistant, receptionist, or secretary. When a call is made to somebody at his or her residence, the gatekeeper may be a spouse. Why does a gatekeeper screen calls for the prospect? Because important people value their time and don't want to talk to every salesperson who calls. It would be an ineffective use of time for a businessperson to talk to every salesperson who called. However, occasionally they will talk to some salespeople. It's your job to see to it that you're one of them!

Michael Baker's initial contact with William Silver is a "cold call," meaning that the two of them have not met previously. Note that Baker refers to his prospect by name rather than asking to speak to the company's chairman. The five sales experts agree that doing your homework in advance includes, among other information, learning the correct name and title of the person whom you wish to speak to.

Baker immediately attempts to assume control of the conversation with the secretary. He must do so because if she asks too many questions, there is a good chance that she will tell him that she'll relay the message to Mr. Silver and "*if* he's interested, *he'll* call back." Baker knows that *he* must be the person who speaks to the prospect—not a disinterested, uninformed third party, in this case the gatekeeper! Otherwise, he could lose the sale even before he's had an opportunity to present his product. Because so many companies are using telemarketing today, businesspeople are besieged by salespeople making cold calls, and it is more difficult than ever to get through to a prospect. To compound the problem, cold calls are even more difficult when a salesperson represents a company whose name is unfamiliar to the general public. (In Baker's case, Winchester Associates is not an immediately recognizable firm.) In some cases, the prestigious reputation of a major company serves as an effective door opener. A call from a marketing rep with Citicorp, Salomon Brothers, Inc., or IBM, for example, is more likely to capture the immediate respect of a gatekeeper, although there are times when representing a well-known company can backfire. It's an immediate tip-off that the caller is selling insurance when he identifies himself as being with Metropolitan Life or Prudential Life, which often is followed with an I'm-not-interested-in-buying-insurance response.

Joe Gandolfo's only objective for using the telephone on a cold call is to set up an appointment. "I never attempt to sell at this stage, nor for that matter do I ever try to sell when I'm making an in-person cold call," he states. "It shows disrespect for the other person's time. It's as if you're saying, 'I don't care what you were doing when I called. Drop it, because what I have to talk to you about is far more important.' At this stage, my one objective is to set up a time for the prospect to hear my presentation. Nothing else."

With this in mind, Gandolfo believes that as little as necessary should be said to the gatekeeper, with the assumption that the call will be put through. For that reason, he simply says, "Hello, this is Joe Gandolfo. Is Mr. Smith in?" Occasionally that's all it takes. Also, sometimes this method can make the gatekeeper think the boss knows the caller and he or she will therefore automatically put him through.

However, when Gandolfo is calling a referral and is asked, "Does Mr. Smith know you?" he says, "Bill Jones suggested that I call Mr. Smith. Kindly put me through to him." Note that Gandolfo, like Baker, authoritatively asks to speak to the prospect.

If it's not a referral, Gandolfo says, "I've been working with people in the automobile industry (or whatever business the prospect is in), and I want to speak with Mr. Smith." Once again, he assertively says, "Kindly put me through to him."

If asked, "What are you selling?" Gandolfo replies, "I'm with ABC Life Insurance company. Kindly put me through to him."

He states that because he speaks with conviction and confidence, he generally isn't asked additional questions and his call is put through. However, in a case when the secretary replies, "I'm sorry, but he's not interested. Mr. Smith has all the insurance he needs," Gandolfo asks, "How do you know? Do you buy his insurance for him?" Once more he says, "Kindly put me through to him."

Another favorite reply to "The boss is not interested" is, "He's not? That's the first time in twenty-seven years I ever heard that." Gandolfo says, "This remark works well because it can really throw them off guard. People often don't know how to react."

If told, "He never talks to a salesman," Gandolfo quickly replies, "Well, then I've *got* to see him. I want to meet somebody who has never talked to a salesman."

The Gandolfo telephone approach is effective for three reasons: (1) he's persistent; (2) he's well prepared with rebuttals at the tip of his tongue; and (3) he's aggressive and controls the interview by not pausing often to give the gatekeeper an opening to ask more questions.

Shafiroff agrees that Baker's directly-to-the-point approach is the best way to handle a gatekeeper. "I believe in presenting myself in a pleasant and authoritative manner. I speak firmly and never hesitate. This self-confidence influences the gatekeeper's reaction. Hopefully, he or she will say to the prospect, 'There's a Mr. Shafiroff on the phone. I'm not sure what he wants, but he sounds important. I think you should talk to him.' However, if the gatekeeper doesn't think the salesperson sounds important, he or she will relay that message, too. 'There's a salesman on the phone. Shall I get rid of him?' As you can see, the initial impression the caller leaves on the gatekeeper is an essential one."

When Shafiroff is asked, "What's the nature of your call?" or, "Does Mr. Jones know you?" he replies, "We haven't met yet, but I'm sure Mr. Jones is familiar with my company. However, my call does not relate to company matters. It's more personal than that." By making it confidential and personal, Shafiroff eliminates a lot of cross-examining by the gatekeeper.

Shafiroff thinks that it's a matter of how you see yourself. "What you must always keep in mind is that your objective is not to leave the decision in the hands of the third party who's screening the prospect's calls. This person should not be permitted to be the one who determines whether the prospect is interested in hearing your message. Regardless of what you sell—real estate, insurance, office equipment, whatever—it's up to the prospect to decide what he is interested in buying.

"Frankly, if a stockbroker feels he's only selling stocks, then fine," Shafiroff continues. "Don't call on Mr. Jones anymore if his secretary tells you that he's not interested in talking to another stockbroker. But it's a matter of personal attitude, and I never felt that I was just another stockbroker. So, I never accepted the fact that because a prospect didn't want to talk to a stockbroker, I was included in that category. I've always believed I had something special to offer: a strategy toward investments that could create greater wealth and personal satisfaction."

Using a relaxed approach with the third party, when cross-examined by a gatekeeper, Shafiroff says, "I want to emphasize that I have nothing specifically in mind for Mr. Jones. My call is more in the manner of a personal introduction. I would appreciate a few moments of his time." With the majority of his calls, Shafiroff has been referred to the new prospect by an existing client, and in those cases he adds, "Bill Miller, a personal friend of Mr. Jones, suggested I call."

For the purpose of maximizing time, sometimes one of Shafiroff's assistants actually places the initial cold call for him. When this is the case, the assistant says, "Mr. Jones please. I have Mr. Martin Shafiroff, managing director with Shearson/Lehman, on the wire." This approach can make the call seem important. In Shafiroff's case, it works for two reasons: (1) he is a managing director with a major investment firm and can use that title to his advantage; (2) someone who has an assistant handling his calls often is perceived as important. To the gatekeeper, there could be a host of reasons why a man in Shafiroff's position would want to speak with his or her boss. Not wanting to offend the caller, a good gatekeeper doesn't want to ask the wrong questions!

Prime prospects for Bettye Hardeman are people who have been referred to her by existing clients—those individuals who have either sold or bought homes through her. "I mostly call prospects in the evening during their nonworking hours," she explains. "This way, I can talk to both the husband and the wife. However, there are times when I must contact somebody at his or her office. In these cases, my approach, like Baker's, is direct: 'This is Bettye Hardeman. May I please speak to Mr. Smith.' Sometimes, the secretary thinks that it's a personal call and puts me through without any resistance. When I'm asked what the nature of my call is, I say, 'Mr. Brown recommended that I call Mr. Smith on a personal matter. May I please speak to him?' When asked, 'What for?' I say, 'It has to do with his home, and it's personal.' Of course, talking about his home is personal, so she's apt to put the call through without any further questioning. A lot of my success has to do with the confidence in my voice. Frankly, the thought that I won't get through never enters my mind."

Buck Rodgers concurs that a salesperson must use the telephone to schedule appointments. "The idea of dropping in unannounced and hoping to see a customer is a waste of time," he contends. While agreeing that Baker's approach is appropriate for him, Rodgers points out that when a salesperson is representing a well-known company, it is quite a different situation and there is often a different approach and a different response.

Typically, Rodgers's first words to the secretary are, "My name is Buck Rodgers, with IBM. I'd like to speak to Mr. Miller." And, as he explains, "The IBM name will at least get me some attention, but it's up to *me* to get my foot in the door."

If there is some resistance, Rodgers says, "Look, I know you haven't met me, and I know your boss is a busy person. I also know that I have something really worthwhile to give her that will help her run her business, and she would want you to provide me with an opportunity to talk to her."

Sometimes the gatekeeper replies, "I'm sorry, but she's busy right now. May I have your number, and I'll have her call you." In this situation, Rodgers tells the gatekeeper, "I know, from having my own secretary, what your job entails. I know it's tough for you to decide whom she speaks to. I also recognize that she's busy, but believe me, what I have to say will be well worth her time. And I know she will appreciate that you gave me a chance to speak with her." Like the

others in the group, Rodgers states that voice, authority, and self-assurance are essential to getting to speak
to the right person.

There is no question that some of the best prospects
are the best guarded. So in order to excel in sales, you
must know how to get through to them.

Creating Initial Interest

Baker's initial contact with Bill Silver is a telephone call to schedule an appointment for the following week. In other situations, a salesperson might first contact a prospect in person.

Mary Kay Ash believes that a salesperson gets only one chance to make a good first impression. For this reason, she thinks that the initial approach to a prospect is the most crucial part of the sales presentation. "All the selling skills in the world won't matter if you don't get your foot in the door," she claims. "By speaking authoritatively, with an air of confidence, Baker makes a statement that he is not a run-of-the-mill salesperson. He is important."

The five sales experts agree that the way in which Baker immediately identifies himself to the prospect is professional and effective. "I like his directness," Hardeman says. "Up front, Baker states his name, the company he represents, and that it specializes in men's custom clothing. Unlike a lot of salesmen, he doesn't beat around the bush."

"He does what I used to do when I first got started in the insurance business," Gandolfo says. "I represented a company called Kennesaw Life Insurance Company, and after I'd introduce myself, I'd say, 'I'm sure you're familiar with Kennesaw Life.' Most people automatically nod their heads in agreement, especially when a salesperson's head is bobbing up and down. Now, I know that the vast majority of people never heard of the company, but by the way I said it, they thought they were *supposed* to know who Kennesaw was."

Gandolfo also likes Baker's appearance and the fact that he wears a Winchester suit. "It's a big mistake for a salesperson not to use the product he sells," the insurance agent states. "It's paramount to a Mercedes salesman driving a Caddy or a Chevy. Unless you believe in your product one hundred percent, you're simply not going to be effective. And I'll tell you something. Before I owned a million dollars of life insurance, I couldn't sell a million-dollar policy because I couldn't understand how anyone could afford so much coverage. Once I was insured for a million, and several more later on, I had the conviction to convince others that they, too, should be insured for those amounts. People sense this kind of conviction the very moment a salesman opens his mouth—whether he's in the same room or on the telephone."

Gandolfo, Shafiroff, and Rodgers are strong advocates of "concept selling" and like the way Baker tells the prospect, "I would like to share an idea with you." Gandolfo, for instance, initially tells a prospect, "I'm in the insurance and tax-shelter business, and I'm assuming that you pay more than four thousand dollars a year in taxes, personal or corporate. If so, you're paying too much and I'd like to run some ideas by you." This statement is a big attention-getter and opens the door with Gandolfo capturing immediate interest. "Who wouldn't be interested if they're paying more than four thousand a year in taxes?" he says. "Of course, I have to substantiate that statement in my presentation."

Likewise, in Shafiroff's initial approach he emphasizes that he deals in values. He stresses, "Wherever those values may be, and in whatever markets those values may be, my main concern is finding them for you. I also concentrate on special situations, seeking out companies with low multiples, high dividends, significant book values, and the possibility of realizing substantial capital gains." Shafiroff explains that he doesn't sell a specific stock during his first contact with a prospect. "I merely introduce myself and talk to him about my investment philosophy to see if it's in harmony with his. If we're not conceptually on the same wave length, then I don't have anything to sell him."

Rodgers points out that the IBM cold-call approach creates initial interest by making a statement: "We're in the business of trying to provide solutions to a variety of different problems. Technology is moving very fast today, and I deal with many companies similar to yours, Mr. Prospect, where the use of our equipment has improved their profits. All we're trying to do at IBM is enhance productivity. For instance, our machines may accomplish this by enabling your volume to grow without having to increase your manpower. However, in order to take advantage of our equipment, there are a few things I have to know about your company." Then, soon into the presentation, a fact-finding session occurs.

During his initial approach, Baker mentions the names of several of his satisfied customers. This is done to establish credibility that his product has been well received by prominent people in the community. The five sales experts agree that this is an important procedure because it lets the prospect know that your product has benefited leading businesspersons who have good judgment. Shafiroff, who still makes it a practice to make six cold calls every day, claims that his best receptions are from those prospects referred to him by his existing clientele. When he mentions, "So-and-so told me to call you, Mr. Prospect," it's like having an introduction that gives him an immediate endorsement. The prospect knows that Shafiroff must have a fine reputation and expertise, because he respects the opinion of the third party.

The first thing that Gandolfo says to a new prospect

is, "Mr. Jones, I'm Joe Gandolfo. Has Bill Miller mentioned my name to you?" Gandolfo explains, "It doesn't make any difference what the prospect answers, this breaks the ice. In fact, even when I don't have a referral, I'll mention the name of one of the prospect's competitors who's a client of mine. Now, it's highly unlikely that his competition would have talked to him about me, but again, it's an icebreaker. And, you can bet that he's interested in knowing what his competitor is up to, so I generally get good reception."

Rodgers explains that when calling on a bank, for example, he says, "I have worked with a number of banking organizations that are similar to your bank in terms of size. These banks have been able to take advantage of IBM equipment in a variety of ways, and I'd like to present some of the uses of our equipment to you." I always make it a point to discuss other customers in the same industry who are working in similar environments. I wouldn't, for example, mention Bank of America or Citicorp to a $100 million bank, because its problems are so different that the prospect won't be able to relate to an organization that's one hundred times bigger. But when I speak about familiar customers who have corrected the same set of problems, I'll get the prospect's immediate attention."

Rodgers also explains that today's IBM marketing reps specialize according to industry. He thinks the days are gone when a salesperson could canvass a territory, calling on a bank, a retailer, a manufacturer, and an insurance company, going down the street calling on business after business. "By your being a specialist, and speaking the customer's language, the businessperson quickly recognizes you as an expert in his problems," Rodgers emphasizes. "By doing this, you create a level of confidence, and he's going to listen to you because he believes you have something to offer him." Another of Rodgers's strong opening lines is, "If I could prove to you that I have some products, some views, and some ideas that are going to help your bottom line and make your business run a little bit better, would you be interested in talking to me?" At the very least, a businessperson is going to say, "Well, go ahead. I'm willing to listen to you."

"Convincing a group of women attending a beauty class at the very beginning of the session that you're an expert in your field," Ash says, "is vital, and you must come across this way immediately in the approach. As I said earlier, it's very important for a beauty consultant to be properly prepared *before* walking into a hostess's home. She must present herself as an authority on beauty, and what better way is there than to *look* the part. Of course, while appearance is essential, you can't sell on looks alone. You've got to know what you're talking about. Now, most women think they're knowledgeable about cosmetics. Don't forget, they've been using all kinds for years. So, it's the job of our beauty consultant to let her audience know she can teach them something at the very start of her presentation. After all, the women attending have been told that she is going to conduct a two-hour beauty class. But if she doesn't capture their attention right at the very beginning, the actual presentation will be a tough, uphill battle. To accomplish this, a beauty consultant explains, 'I've had extensive training in skin care and cosmetics, and I'm fully qualified to conduct this class. I can assure you that you'll learn many things about your skin today that you previously didn't know. And I'll be delighted to answer any questions that you may have.'"

Regarding the content of the letter Baker sends to his prospects prior to the first sales interview, this can vary, depending on the type of company one works for. In the case of IBM and Mary Kay Cosmetics, it simply isn't necessary to send anything other than the confirmation letter itself. Both companies are so well recognized throughout America that they don't need an introduction. However, in the cases of Shafiroff and Gandolfo, even though they do represent well-known companies, they are, in their own right, "superstars" and like to promote themselves rather than the firms they represent. This is valuable in their respective fields because they compete with other stockbrokers and insurance agents even within the organizations for which they sell. As Shafiroff puts it, "By enclosing my personal biosketch and several magazine and newspaper articles that have featured me, I provide something tangible to the prospect that adds a new dimension to the relationship. Rather than simply sending him a brochure about my company and some general information about the securities industry, I personalize it, and at the same time the articles express something about my investment philosophy."

Gandolfo also sends literature and articles about him that have appeared in many prestigious publications. "I believe in selling myself during my initial approach both by mail and in person," he says. "I don't hesitate to inform a prospect that in many circles I'm considered the number one life insurance agent in the world. I have a ritual of putting my business card on the prospect's desk and saying, 'There are more than four hundred thousand life insurance agents and financial counselors on the face of this earth, and I think it's important for you to know about my qualifications for coming here in the first place. If you'll permit me, I'd like to tell you something about myself,' and then I do! I recommend that other salespeople do this too. What does this accomplish? I'm letting the prospect know that he's dealing with a professional, that's what! It tells him that you're different from the run-of-the-mill person in the business."

Hardeman does not send literature about her status as America's number one residential real estate agent. Although many articles have been published about her success, she sends only facts and maps about the residential market in the Atlanta area. "Sure, I know it's good PR to let them know about me in advance," she says, "but I don't feel comfortable doing it. I just don't like to toot my own horn.

"My main emphasis to create initial interest is telling a prospect, 'I know the Atlanta market like the back of my hand, and I'll work with you as long as it takes to find you a home.' I just try to make a prospect feel so comfortable with me that he won't want to do business with anyone else."

The Fact-Finding
Session

A major portion of Baker's presentation is concerned with *fact finding* about the prospect. During this period, Baker asks dozens of detailed questions *prior* to showing his merchandise in order to find out what the individual's needs are.

The five sales experts all believe that Baker's fact-finding session is the most professional way to sell a product and get an order. All of them do this—an interesting phenomenon, considering the differences in their product lines (computers, cosmetics, insurance, real estate, and securities).

While the obvious reason to conduct a fact-finding session is to obtain knowledge about the prospect's needs, Shafiroff thinks it also enables him to "qualify" a prospect. "It's a time-saver because it helps me eliminate people who are not potential customers," he states. Likewise, Hardeman believes it permits her to find out how large a mortgage a prospect can qualify for, which is important because financing is a major factor in the purchasing of real estate.

Each sales expert believes that it's imperative to know the prospect's needs before attempting to make a sale. "Otherwise, you're working in the dark," Ash explains. In the case of skin care and cosmetics, there are several different factors that a beauty consultant must know before she can determine what to sell to whom. Before the actual sales presentation, our representative calls each prospect who will be attending the skin-care class (a group sales presentation) and says, 'I want to be certain that I'm familiar with your type of skin so I can best serve you on——(day of class). May I ask you a few questions?' Then she proceeds to ask questions from a 'beauty profile'; it's a form with a carbon copy that was developed by our research department. It asks scientific questions in lay terminology to determine the type of skin each person has, and which of our three formulas is most suitable for her. The form is also presented to groups of women at beauty shows; after they have answered the questions by checking boxes, our beauty consultant has considerable information on five or six people simultaneously."

While the actual questions differ in each sales expert's warm-up session, there are similarities in the information they seek. The following are sample questions asked by each member of the panel.

MARY KAY ASH

- How does your skin feel six hours after you have applied your makeup?
- Does your face feel dry in the morning when you wake up?
- How does your face feel when you wake up in the morning?

"We never actually ask a prospect if her skin is dry or oily," Ash explains, "because so often, she doesn't know. However, all of the questions are designed to determine the type of skin she has, so our beauty consultant knows which of our cosmetics and skin-care products to recommend."

MARTIN SHAFIROFF

- What are your objectives [financial]?
- What do you want to accomplish?
- Are you interested in capital gains or income?
- Tell me about your past investments, taking into consideration what you're seeking now.
- How do you feel about tax-free municipals?
- What is your thinking about the so-called glamour stocks selling at high multiples?
- What size investment would you be comfortable with?

"I start off asking general questions," Shafiroff explains, "and then I progress into more personal ones. Over a period of time, I'll ask him questions about how he became successful, how he achieved what he has, what qualities got him there, and what advice he'd recommend for somebody just starting in his field. Still later, I'll ask questions about his family, his hobbies, his recreations, and so on. I'm always interested in learning what makes my client tick, and I can't find out too much about him. I develop different relationships with people I do business with; some are more receptive to opening up than others. With some, I can get very personal, and sometimes it's strictly a business relationship. It all depends on the individual."

JOE GANDOLFO

- How much insurance do you now have?
- How old are you?
- Tell me about your health.
- Tell me about your family.
- What are your present earnings?
- Tell me about your occupation.
- Do you have any strong feelings about life insurance?

- What financial formula did you use to arrive at your present coverage on your life?
- What do you think about life insurance as an investment?
- What do you think about buying life insurance strictly for protection?
- What about as a savings for you and/or your children's education?
- How about as a source to be used for retirement?
- What do you think about your wife being insured?
- How about your children?
- What do you think about mortgage insurance?
- How do you feel about pension plans using life insurance?
- What is your feeling about using life insurance as liquid dollars to pay federal estate taxes?

Gandolfo states that he never approaches a prospect with any preconceived ideas about what to sell him. "The only way I can find out what his needs are is by asking a lot of questions," he explains. "I don't think a salesperson should ever assume anything until he asks enough questions to understand the customer's needs. I go through my warm-up session with every prospect before I even attempt to sell him a policy. And, most important, I *listen* after I ask each question. Too many salespersons aren't really sincerely interested in hearing how the prospect replies. I truly care. It's vital for a salesperson to understand that selling is a form of two-way communication. You mustn't attempt to dominate the conversation. After I ask a question, I shut up and allow my client to speak. Sometimes I wait for several minutes. I don't feel threatened by the silence. Too many salespersons can't stand the pause in the conversation, and they don't give their prospects enough time to reflect how they think. People resent being treated like that, and they feel high-pressured. When this happens, they resist the salesperson, and no matter how they feel about his product, they don't buy."

BETTYE HARDEMAN

- What kind of home are you interested in?
- Tell me about your family.
- Do you have children?
- What are their ages?
- How important is the school district where you live?
- Tell me about your occupation.
- What price range are you thinking about?
- Do you want a one-story or two-story home?
- How important is the size of the yard?
- Is public transportation important to you?
- What style of home do you like? Colonial? Victorian? Contemporary? Early American? Ranch?
- Do you like older homes or newer homes?
- How many bedrooms are you interested in?
- Do you want a basement? A family room?
- Do you own your present home?
- How much equity do you have in it?

"There's no way in the world I'd know where to begin to show a home to someone without first conducting a fact-finding session," Hardeman says. "There are so many variables that I must find out, and the best way to get the necessary information is by asking a lot of questions. I sell homes to all kinds of people, and without cross-examining a potential home buyer I'd never know where to begin. Someone might want a quiet, secluded lot, for example, and another person wants a friendly neighborhood. One prospect wants an acre, while another would like to have a small lot. An older home turns one couple on, but it has no appeal whatsoever to another couple. As you can see, buying a home is a very personal thing, and it's my job to find the right home for the right buyer. Also, with most people, a home represents their largest investment, so they want to be absolutely certain they get the most value for their money. And, depending upon their needs, what has value to one individual may not be significant to somebody else. Only when I know what appeals to people can I match them up with the right home.

"I never ask too many questions on the phone. I think it's always better to ask questions of a personal nature face-to-face. I believe that any prospect who takes the time to call me is worth giving my time to, so I don't attempt to qualify people on the phone."

BUCK RODGERS

- Tell me about your business.
- What are you trying to accomplish?
- Where would you like your business to be five years from now?
- How long does it take for you to process an order?
- How long would you like it to take?
- What kind of inventory problems do you currently have?
- How long does it take to process your payroll?
- What are your current volumes?
- What is your manufacturing plant's turnover ratio?

"When it comes to selling computers, it's essential to understand that we don't sell a product per se. We sell what a product will do. We're in the business of finding solutions to the customer's problems, and in order to accomplish this, we must understand his business and put together a cost-justified proposal that provides value. The best way to make a sale in this business is to identify the customer's problem by asking him a lot of questions. This means you must be able to answer the question: 'What will your product actually do to make things better?'

"A computer system isn't purchased, for example, because a customer is interested in owning a new piece of machinery. A computer aids in the decision-making process. It frees people from repetitive work. It permits

business to increase the turnover of its inventory. It's
n efficient way to monitor accounts receivable. In med-
:ine, a computer helps save lives. There are countless
·ays a computer can serve the customer, and at IBM,
1e success of a marketing rep is dependent upon his
bility to be application oriented. This means he must
rst understand what a customer's problems are before
e can intelligently begin to solve them. It's a matter of
rep doing enough fact finding to fully understand
·hat is giving the prospect the greatest challenges.
•nce this is identified, the rep can begin to take the
ppropriate IBM equipment and put it in the prospect's
ffice, factory, or perhaps warehouse, and provide a
·lution to his problem. But the rep can't very well
1swer any problems unless he's able to draw out the
ecessary day-to-day bits of information from the pros-
ect. As you can see, a lot of fact finding is required
efore an IBM rep can properly do his or her job."

While all five sales experts conduct fact-finding ses-
ons, the length of time of these sessions varies consid-
·ably. At first blush, one would expect the product's
·rice tag to be the number one factor in determining
1e time involvement (a salesperson would spend less
·me questioning a cosmetics prospect than would a real
state agent or a computer rep). And, while it is true
1at Mary Kay Cosmetics salespeople conduct the
·riefest fact-finding sessions, Hardeman, who sells homes,
nd Shafiroff, who sells stocks that sometimes have six-
nd seven-figure price tags, spend less time than
:andolfo spends selling insurance and Rodgers spends
· computer sales. "IBM fact-finding missions take con-
.derably longer than an hour or two," Rodgers points
ut. "In fact, we may spend weeks or months analyzing
roblems and facts before we install a new system or put
· a new application. It's not simply a matter of asking
>mebody, 'What's your problem?' We put in consider-
ble preparation making sure we select the right product

for each customer. But, when you stop to consider that the guts of the prospect's business is dependent on his computer systems, we've got to be absolutely certain we're doing the best possible job for him. We've got to get all the facts because we can't afford to make a mistake."

Baker listens after asking questions during the fact-finding session. "It's important that the prospect doesn't feel he's being cross-examined," Shafiroff comments, "and I like the way Baker conducts a two-way conversation. He does it quite naturally and makes the prospect feel at ease. It's poor selling when a sales presentation becomes a one-way conversation, dominated by the salesperson." Ash says, "Too often, many salespeople tend to forget that listening is an essential part of communication. They pay little attention to what the prospect says, and consequently miss many buying signals. It's vital to hear the prospect's thoughts during the fact-finding session. In fact, during this part of the sales presentation more time should be devoted to listening than to talking. That's why God gave us two ears and one mouth. I think he expects us to listen twice as much as we speak."

Ash likens the fact-finding session to a first visit with a doctor: "A physician who asks you a lot of questions shows that he cares about your health. But the doctor who seems too busy to ask enough questions to diagnose the problem gives you the impression that he really doesn't care; he's only interested in his fee. 'When did you first begin to have this pain in your back?' a caring doctor asks. 'What were you doing at the time?' 'Tell me what you ate just before you noticed the pain.' 'Does it hurt much when I touch you right here? How about here?' 'Does it hurt when you lie down? When you walk up stairs?' By taking the time to listen to his patient's comments, a doctor demonstrates his genuine concern. Similarly, when a salesperson listens carefully to what the prospect says, he shows that his reason for being there isn't solely to make a commission."

Gandolfo believes that by being a good listener, Baker generates confidence, "because he demonstrates sincerity in his desire to understand the other person's needs."

Hardeman says, "During the fact-finding session, I let my prospect talk just as long as he feels like it. It relaxes him and lets him know that I truly have his best interest at heart."

Finally, Rodgers concludes, "It's simply a matter of respect for the other person to let him have his say. Unfortunately, too many salespeople forget to extend this basic courtesy during a sales presentation. Many sales organizations are so concerned about teaching their salespeople how to present their product that they fail to give them any instructions on the art of listening, which can't be emphasized enough."

Presenting
the Product

Only after Baker spends considerable time conducting a fact-finding session does he actually present his product. And at this time he doesn't show suits, but instead displays swatches of fabrics and patterns. This is his "demonstration," just as an automobile salesperson sells his product by having the prospect sit behind the wheel and take the car for a spin.

"Even though a piece of material representing a fine men's suit is far different from a house," Hardeman says, "I liken Baker's presentation to mine because he shows only a small selection of swatches at a time for his prospect to choose from. That's how I sell homes! After I've conducted my fact-finding session, I am able to determine what areas of Atlanta in the prospect's price range are most suitable. Then, with an out-of-town couple, for instance, I'll take them around to see different neighborhoods. Once they know what part of town they like best, I must find out what type of home, how much yard they want, and so on. I can then narrow it down to a relatively small number of homes in a given area that best match a family's needs. This way, I don't have to run all over the county showing them homes that they would never consider. Not only would I be wasting their time and mine, but I'd only confuse them.

By showing his prospect only a small selection of swatches at a time, I believe Baker is right on target.

"Now, of course, when I show a home, there's no resemblance between what I do and Baker's presentation. Remember, I have to physically walk the prospect through a house and yard. I can't do it sitting in somebody's office! I always start by entering the front door because it offers the best over-all view of the house. And, like Baker, who analyzed his prospect's needs by careful listening during the fact-finding session, I, too, know which points of the home to stress. With most people, it's the kitchen and bathrooms. With others, it's the family room and the master bedroom. Naturally, it fluctuates from customer to customer, and no two homes are alike. So, I emphasize different features of a home according to the needs of the prospect."

In some ways, a Mary Kay skin-care class resembles Baker's "demonstration." Just as Baker must analyze his client's physical appearance, a beauty consultant must analyze each woman's beauty profile before she presents different shades of makeup. The profile is based on a five-year research program on seven thousand women that focuses on the basic skin colors: ivory, beige, and bronze. Ash explains that if a woman went to four different so-called color analysts, spending about a hundred dollars on each, it's possible she would get four conflicting opinions on whether she was a "summer, spring, winter, or fall" coloration and might be told that much of her wardrobe was absolutely wrong for her! Instead of telling a woman to change her wardrobe to match her coloration, a Mary Kay glamour cosmetics presentation demonstrates how a woman can wear any color simply by changing her makeup! There are different "cool" and "warm" colors for eye shadow, lip colors, and blushers, and a beauty consultant can spin her color wheel to match up the correct shades to complement the customer's outfit. As is the case with Baker, once it's learned what the prospect's colors are, it's simply a matter of educating the prospect on what goes with what. A beauty consultant uses charts and forms (the beauty profile), because she makes a group presentation to five or so women, who are asked to select different merchandise. For this reason, she instructs each member of the class to fill in her own form based on her individual beauty profile; each person gets a different result tailor-made to fit her special needs. Only when she closes the sale does the consultant speak to each prospect individually. At this point, she answers their personal questions.

Gandolfo, Rodgers, and Shafiroff are strong supporters of concept selling. Consequently, each devotes a major portion of his presentation to securing agreement on the need that his product fills before specifically focusing on its nuts and bolts. Both Gandolfo and Shafiroff sell intangible products, so neither can actually give a demonstration (you can't physically show how a thousand shares of XYZ Company increase in value, nor can you show how a life insurance policy works when somebody dies—you can only describe what happens). Keep in mind, however, that Baker only shows swatches—he doesn't show an actual Winchester suit, with the exception of the one he's wearing.

"The product I sell is nothing more than a piece of paper—a legal document with features such as nonforfeiture options, settlement options, and automatic premium loans," Gandolfo points out. "It's an agreement whereupon the insurer will pay the beneficiary of the insured a certain sum of money in consideration of a specific amount of money paid on an annual basis. Of course, there's more to it than this, but you get the picture. If I went through the motions of taking out an actual insurance policy, which is an insurance agent's product, and read and explained it to a prospect, I'd starve to death in this business. I present what an insurance policy will do for someone. So my job is to present ideas on how my product will benefit the prospect or, in the event of his death, the person(s) designated as his beneficiary. For instance, when I sell a

$300,000 policy to a thirty-year old man, I explain to him how he can provide for his wife and two children if he dies prematurely. Another $300,000 policy—the identical product—may be sold to another client for a business purpose such as a buy-sell agreement to provide the necessary funds for a surviving partner to acquire the deceased's interest in the business. As you can see, when I demonstrate my product, the prospect never sees the actual contract that he ultimately will own. Instead, it's my job to create a mental picture of the desperate situation that can occur if he doesn't buy—and the positive alternative if he does buy. Baker, too, presents a mental picture by making his prospect visualize himself in a fine suit. If he can't create that image, his prospect isn't going to buy. After all, nobody spends five hundred dollars for a swatch of a suit's material."

"I talk about investment philosophies with my prospect," Shafiroff says, "before I attempt to sell him on taking a position in a specific company. One prospect, for example, might be interested in the income that his investment can generate. Another wants to preserve his capital; he wants it to appreciate at a higher rate than inflation. And, above all, I know that every prospect is interested in value. Initially, I only talk about concepts, not about how much to invest in what. Only after the prospect's philosophy has been established do I discuss the subject of what investment will fulfill his needs. For the person interested in income, I might present an investment in a company where there is a significant and growing cash dividend. With somebody who demonstrates a concern for preservation of capital, I might present a low multiple company with significant assets that offer an opportunity for substantial appreciation.

"When I finally discuss a particular product, I'll say, I think XYZ Corporation makes a lot of sense, John. Do you know any other company selling at five times earnings with a twenty percent return on equity? The company has four hundred million in working capital, and its book value is substantially higher than the market value. Could we duplicate this company at two or more times its present market price? The answer is no.' Then, after giving him several reasons why it's a good investment, I say, 'John, I feel that you should own ten thousand shares of XYZ.' "

Demonstrating a large computer system is a far cry from demonstrating the products sold by the other sales experts. As Rodgers explains, "A sale of a large system can take place over a period of months. Just the fact-finding session alone may involve sending several IBM support people to various customer locations. Now, the actual demonstration of how a large computer system works can't be shown in the customer's place of business. Only with a small unit, such as a personal computer, can it be carried in, as we'd do to give a typewriter or copier demonstration. We can't ship a large computer system in because of the high costs of running cables underneath the floor, installing special air-conditioning, and so on.

"For this reason, we must take the prospect somewhere else to demonstrate a computer system. It can take place at several different locations. For example, IBM has industry meetings on the order of a convention where hundreds of customers are brought in. At these meetings, we ship several different machines in so we can conduct demonstrations for many customers in individual and group presentations. Other times, we'll bring a prospective customer to one of our facilities. We have many education centers and application centers that serve this purpose. There's a facility at our banking center in Raleigh, for instance, that's set up like the inside of a bank. It even has people who act as loan officers and pension officers. There, the prospect actually views the specialized equipment performing various banking functions that he can relate to his own bank's needs.

"And what I believe is the highest form of marketing," Rodgers continues, "are those presentations where we *showcase a customer*. By 'showcasing' I mean we

ake a prospect to a satisfied customer's location and
how him a specific application being performed, and
e sees the end result of it. Baker does this in a minor
vay when he mentions satisfied customers who wear
Winchester suits. He attempts to paint a mental picture
or his prospect, enabling him to visualize familiar,
vell-groomed business leaders. In the case of an IBM
omputer, which frequently contains the guts of a large
usiness, more than a visualization is required. So,
fter getting permission from a satisfied customer, we
emonstrate a live environment. The prospect now has
n opportunity to ask questions, and he can personally
iew how a problem similar to his own has been solved
y our equipment."

A final phase in the presentation of a complicated sale
might involve making a formal proposal, complete with
ip charts and slides. Included might be a projection of
ost savings, an orderly timetable for educating and
raining people, an installation schedule if called for, a
esting of the equipment, and the cost of the system.
he timetable is called a "pert chart," which is a step-
y-step series of different events that occurs over a
eriod of time until the entire program is implemented.
n short, the prospect is told, "I'm going to lay out the
xact series of detailed events that will take place,
omplete with all checkpoints and procedures." The
rospect knows exactly what to expect, and because
here will be no surprises, he will feel comfortable
oing business with the company.

Finally, a product's cost, complexity, effect on the
vork and/or personal life of the customer, and the
ustomer's familiarity with it are obviously significant
actors that determine how much detail and what length
f time are required to present a product. For instance,
he decision-making process for the purchase of a piece
f costume jewelry would consume less time than that
or an expensive diamond necklace. In the case of the
iamond necklace, a person might read some books
nd/or articles about the diamond market, carefully re-

search the quality of the stones, inquire about the jeweler's reputation, and do some comparison shopping.

Price by itself doesn't necessitate a drawn-out sales presentation. For instance, a large securities transaction in the high six-figure or seven-figure range might be concluded during a fifteen-minute telephone conversation. Yet, the purchase of a $50,000 home might take weeks or months to decide. Although the home might not be complex, the decision to purchase a residence is apt to have a greater impact on one's life. Also, familiarity with the product is a factor that determines how much explanation and detail must be given to make a sale. For this reason, a $5 million life insurance policy might be sold to a sophisticated buyer more quickly than a $20,000 policy to someone else; a $100 million sale of commercial real estate might take less time to present than a $100,000 property; and the same applies to a large stock transaction versus a small one, and so on. As you can see, each product has its differences, and there are so many variables. Each must be presented in its own unique way, but the basic selling principles are the same.

Controlling
the Sale

At first blush, controlling the sale has a negative connotation implying manipulation of a prospect. But, in this context, controlling the sale means maintaining a posture of authority, in the same manner as a consultant directs a client, a physician advises a patient, or a clergyman guides a parishioner. A salesperson should control a sales interview in the same manner as a fine stage actor captivates his audience or a superb conductor leads his orchestra. Because, when done properly, that's exactly what happens. The professional salesperson *directs, advises, guides, captivates, and leads.*

Throughout the sale, Baker has many techniques to execute control, such as in the beginning when *he* determines where he will sit, to the end, when he instructs the prospect how to make out his check! Does the prospect resent a salesperson for it? If executed with perfection, he shouldn't.

Gandolfo believes that in *any* relationship involving two people, there is always one who exerts more control than the other. "This applies to husbands and wives, brothers and sisters, friends, everyone," he says. "So, if someone must be in control during a sales presentation, I'm in favor of it being the salesperson.

"It's a matter of directing the prospect's mind so he

can make a buying decision in an orderly manner," Gandolfo continues. "I think it's essential to keep his mind focused on what I say. If his thoughts drift, then I might lose him. Sometimes, a prospect might try to sidetrack me because he is consciously or subconsciously avoiding making a decision to buy. He may offer me a cup of coffee, a cigarette, or perhaps attempt to start a conversation about some mounted sailfish on his office wall. Some salespeople fall for the trap and accept friendly gestures, hoping to score a few 'points.' I don't buy that! It wouldn't matter if I were dying of thirst, I wouldn't accept a glass of water offered to me during a presentation. Because if I did, I'd risk losing control of the sale! Anything that's not directly related to the prospect's buying from me is a distraction that I avoid. I never forget my sole objective for being there—I'm there to make a sale, and if I lose control, my chances are reduced."

Baker is good at giving "little orders" to his prospect. Even if Silver happens to realize that Baker is controlling the sale in this manner, it is done in a way that will not offend him. For instance, when Baker asks for a swatch number, he orders, "Read it to me, will you please?" He does it again when he says, "Feel that fabric"; "Stand back. I want you to see . . ."; "Face that way . . ."; "Let your arm down . . ."; "Inhale . . ."; "Exhale . . . " Bettye Hardeman does the same thing when she shows a prospect a home. "For instance," she says, "I might walk to the window with a prospect in order for him to get a good view of the outdoor scenery. I might even suggest that we take a stroll through the grounds. Then, too, I might tactfully suggest for someone to come with me to a particular room that had already been viewed. Sure, this is a form of control, but I don't actually 'order' people around like some salespeople do to control the sale. It's just not my style. I'm always courteous, and by nature I happen to be a soft-spoken person. Yet, in my own quiet way, I'm able to maintain control. It's just that I don't come across as being overly aggressive—and frankly, I think most prospects dislike real estate agents who push too hard.

"I usually drive my car," Hardeman adds. "And again, it's a form of controlling the sale. You know, it puts me in the driver's seat. But that's not really my reason for doing it. I just know the area better than the prospect, particularly an out-of-towner."

A Mary Kay beauty consultant sets the stage for her presentation, according to Ash, by arranging the hostess's living-room table for displaying her merchandise in advance of the actual beauty class. This is similar to what Baker does when he sits down and nods for his prospect to do the same. She is the one who determines who sits where during a presentation. A beauty consultant will spend approximately twenty minutes to get things in order before the women arrive at the hostess's home, and she tells each woman where to sit, while she stands at the head of the table. The hostess is told that she mustn't serve refreshments until later—after the class—for it interferes with the makeup process. She also obtains each woman's name in advance and tries to memorize all of them. It's been said that the most beautiful sound in the world is that of a person's own name . . . correctly pronounced.

Ash feels it's particularly important for a salesperson to maintain control of a sale during a group presentation. This type of selling differs from one-on-one selling because the greater the number of people, the more difficult it is to keep their attention. Then, too, with a group, eye contact is obviously less effective. If a salesperson is not able to control them, he or she is likely to end up with a room full of people all thinking on different wave lengths. For this reason, it is imperative to employ certain sales techniques to control a group.

"Note that I said a beauty consultant *stands* at the head of the table while the other women are seated," Ash says. "She doesn't sit down with the guests to make them feel she is 'one of the gang.' This way, she creates a classroom atmosphere—one where the teacher stands at the head of the class facing the students. She assumes a leadership role, and she instructs them on personal skin care and cosmetics. She informs her class, 'Your hostess has allowed me two hours today, and I would like your undivided attention. I also want to answer any questions you may have. So when you leave here, you'll go home feeling that you've learned a lot about your own personal skin care and your coloration.' I believe controlling a group is essential, and in order to do it properly, you must establish control immediately. If not, it becomes increasingly more difficult to obtain it as you continue further into your presentation."

An even more difficult scenario than a group presentation for controlling the sale is selling over the telephone. With Shafiroff, every transaction is a telephone sale! "In my selling," he explains, "I have no eye contact, nor can I employ facial expressions or body language to get someone's attention. My prospect can't see my product, a presentation book, or a chart to keep his mind focused on the sale. I can't even let him touch anything! And who knows what distractions may be going on in his office while I'm selling him! The only two things I can use to hold his attention are my delivery and my message.

"I find that by varying my speech—sometimes talking slower and other times faster, and by raising and lowering my voice—there is a dramatic difference in the reaction I get on the other end of the wire. Sometimes, for example, I'll pause for a moment or so in the middle of a thought, and it's amazing how most people react to silence. They don't want to interrupt, so they just wait. Of course, my pause isn't more than a few seconds, but to the other person it seems much longer. I know that some people seem to think it's a weakness in a conversation when there's a silence. I don't agree. A conversation doesn't have to be nonstop. And it's important to realize that, from a selling point of view, pausing is a very effective technique to get someone's undivided attention. When the prospect is so enthralled with your presentation that you've got him hanging on every word you say, *that's* control."

A technique Shafiroff finds effective is to ask questions that invite the prospect to respond. For example, he'll make a statement and say, "Does this make any sense to you?" or, "What do *you* think about . . ." Each of his questions requires more than a yes or no answer, so the customer has to express an opinion; it's a way of drawing the prospect into the conversation. When Shafiroff is doing a telephone presentation, he must get feedback to know if the prospect is still there. Again, Shafiroff's questions are meant to guide him, so that he can stay in control of the interview.

"The consequences are obvious when a salesperson loses control on the telephone," Shafiroff says. "The other party can abruptly slam the receiver down and end the conversation! In a split second, he can cut you off. In general, people's poorest manners surface both quicker and more frequently on the telephone than when you're face to face with them. Why? Because it's so easy to hang up the phone versus asking somebody seated across the desk to leave your office."

Baker involved Silver in his sales presentation and thereby controlled the sale. Baker conducted a two-way conversation and, at times, even had Silver doing physical things, such as reading the swatch numbers to him; feeling the fabric; standing back to observe the subtleness of the plaid swatch; and going through all sorts of motions while Baker took his measurements. Similarly, Ash, Hardeman, and Rodgers, who sell tangible products, get their prospects to actively participate. Hardeman does it by taking her clients through a house—"In my case, I actually put them inside the product!" she says. "Sometimes, I'll walk for miles in the process of showing several homes to one prospect. I have them walking through every room in the house, climbing up and down stairs from the basement to the attic, and hiking through yards. Sometimes, I'll even suggest that someone stand in a large shower stall to see how roomy it is.

I do this so the person will start feeling what it would be like if he lived in the home. I'll ask my purchaser to stand behind the sink, walk over to the oven, and then to the refrigerator, again to get a feel of what it's like to live in the home. I want my prospects to do a lot more than simply look at things! If there's a nice garden, I'll tell them to take a deep breath and smell the beautiful flowers. I'll also suggest, 'Open the door and see how solid and heavy it is,' and, 'Listen to the birds singing, and the brook bubbling. Won't that be nice to wake up to each morning?' I want them to see, touch, feel, and hear the house.'

At a Mary Kay beauty class, the women are asked in advance to wear a low-neck casual dress, "so that if something is spilled, it won't matter," Ash says. "Women love to play with makeup, and in a beauty class, everyone is participating in doing what the consultant tells the group to do. The first thing a woman is told to do when she sits down at the table is to take off her makeup—naturally, with Mary Kay cleansing cream. At a skin-care class, we teach them things like how to apply a mask and to use our skin freshener. Everyone follows the instructions given by the consultant and she guides them on what to do. The same routine is followed during the cosmetic application in the 'glamour' portion of the beauty class. It's amazing how a woman comes to a beauty class with no intention of participating. Sometimes, in the beginning she will say such things as, 'I'm too old,' 'I'm too ugly, and there's nothing you can do about it.' We coax her gently and say, 'Oh please try it. Your face will feel so soft and nice. I'm sure you'll love it.' After she's finally persuaded to give it a try, and as the class proceeds, she becomes so intrigued that an hour later it's difficult to pry the mirror from her hands. The difference is so striking, and she feels so good about herself. If we just showed some flip-up charts and slides about skin care and cosmetics, our sales presentation wouldn't be nearly as effective. I strongly believe that a salesperson should get the prospect into the act as much as possible. We employ four of the five senses—sight, touch, smell, and hearing."

IBM prospects also participate. As mentioned earlier, they are invited to support centers and industry conferences as well as to other customers' businesses to observe demonstrations. Customer seminars are also conducted on a variety of subjects ranging from how to program computers to how to manage a business. "If the prospect will be the actual operator of the machine," Rodgers explains, "we'll suggest, 'Why don't you sit down here and key in your name here.' This approach works especially well when a personal computer, a typewriter, or a word processor is being demonstrated. With a larger system, however, the main objective is to provide an understanding of how the product works. Also, when a presentation is being made to a company president or financial officers, it may not be appropriate to put them in the seat of a system operator. At this level, the decision maker will not be the user of the machine."

A close observation of the five sales experts reveals that each of them projects a strong image of professionalism. The prospects quickly realize that they are dealing with an expert. Nobody has to tell them. It's obvious by their manner in what and how they present themselves.

Baker knows the clothing business, and his clients quickly realize it. Not only does his self-confidence convey that he's an expert in his field, but it becomes very evident by the way he replies to every question asked of him.

Gandolfo, Hardeman, and Shafiroff all agree that by demonstrating how much they know in their respective fields, it doesn't take long before a prospect's respect is gained, and, like the commercial says, "People listen when I advise them," Shafiroff quips. "There isn't anything a prospect could ask me about life insurance that I couldn't answer," Gandolfo states. "When people believe they're dealing with an expert, it's a lot easier to gain control of the sale. They *want* you to advise them. Hence, they're happy to let you have control. It's when a salesperson doesn't know what he's talking about that people resent being controlled by him. In that case, anyone would offer resistance."

Rodgers concurs that the best way to maintain control of a sale is by demonstrating that you're an expert in your business as well as his. "When you exemplify excellence, the customer is eager to find out what you can do to offer solutions to his or her particular problems," he says. "In addition, it helps to speak the customer's language, as well as to couple your expertise with a genuine interest in helping the customer. Sure, the customer knows you have to make some sort of a quota and get paid a commission, but you must be convincing that it's not just money that's your motivation. Only when you do this can you begin to build a real customer relationship."

Finally, Shafiroff believes that you must have conviction in what you sell. He believes that a customer instinctively knows whether you believe in your product. If you do, they believe in you. "Only then can you really control the sale," he explains.

Assuming
the Sale

Assuming the sale is certainly one of the most common selling techniques. Yet, most people do not recognize it when they are buying, and sometimes even the sellers don't know that they are using this technique. It's so common that we see it every day, For example, when a gasoline attendant asks, "Fill it up?" he's assuming that you not only want gas but want the maximum your tank can hold!

Have you ever noticed how the car-rental agencies assume that you want to purchase collision insurance? They are so presumptive that they have you sign the papers *only if you don't buy it!* Some book-of-the-month clubs require you to notify them only when you don't want to buy a book during a particular month, and the magazine publishers require you write to them in order to discontinue your trial subscription. Why? Because they want inertia on their side—in these cases, it's easier to buy something than *not* to make the purchase.

Then, too, insurance companies assume that you want to renew your policy when they send you a premium invoice. Notice that they don't write to you offering an option on whether you want it for the coming year. Once you're on the books, they assume you're their customer for life, and they keep right on billing you until the day you die! It happens all the time, and often people never notice what is happening.

Baker, too, assumes the sale many times during his presentation. It's a selling technique that's used again and again in conjunction with other selling techniques. Note how it's used by Baker in the following examples:

Getting Past the Gatekeeper: By saying, "Bill Silver, please," instead of asking, "May I please speak to Mr. Silver?" Baker assumes that the gatekeeper will automatically put his call through.

Creating Initial Interest: By saying, "You're familiar with Winchester Associates, aren't you?" Baker assumes that Silver knows his company.

When Baker asks, "Would next Tuesday at eight-fifteen or Wednesday at two forty-five be convenient to see you?" it's assumed that the prospect is agreeable to seeing him at one of these times.

Baker doesn't wait to be offered a seat. He automatically sits down and begins his presentation.

The Fact-Finding Session: Baker doesn't ask permission to conduct his fact-finding session by saying, "Do you mind if I ask you some questions?" He assumes that it's permissible to ask questions.

Furthermore, by the nature of the questions he asks, he is assuming that Silver will ultimately buy. For what other reason would he be interested in such information?

Presenting the Product:

Baker asks the prospect to read the swatch numbers to him while he writes them down on the order pad. Each time he does this, he assumes Silver is making a purchase. Why else would he want to write down swatch numbers of fabrics that the prospect selects?

Controlling the Sale:

As previously discussed, throughout the presentation, Baker maintains control of the sale. Often, while controlling the sale he is also assuming the sale. For example, he goes through a long series of questions while taking Silver's measurements, giving small orders such as, "Put your arms down"; "Turn around"; "Take a deep breath"; and so on. Again, he's obviously assuming the sale, because there is no reason to otherwise conduct such an exercise!

Closing the Sale:
Throughout the entire close, Baker assumes that Silver will buy. This is evident in many ways. For example: "Do you want to pay by check or credit card?" Here, he assumes that he will pay one of two ways. Note that the question is never, "Do you want to buy?"

All of our sales experts also assume the sale at various stages of their presentations. In the case of Mary Kay, when a beauty consultant is attempting to secure a beauty class with a hostess, she will ask, "Would the first part of the week or the latter part of the week be best for you?" It's always a question of something *and something else*, never a choice between something and nothing. For instance, it would be poor selling to ask, "Would you like to have a beauty show?" The answer would probably be no. But the question, "Is there any reason why you couldn't have a beauty show?" generally evokes a yes response. And then the consultant adds a compliment; "I think you'd be terrific." By asking her to give a reason why she couldn't have a show, the prospect is forced to think of an objection. It's much easier for her to simply say yes.

As Baker does, in making an appointment the salesperson should give the prospect a choice of possible appointment times rather than ask him a direct question such as, "Would you like to meet with me at nine A.M. so I could sell you a new car?" If it was put that way, there would be very few sales made.

Gandolfo's approach also assumes that the prospect will consent to see him when given the choice. Often his approach is, "I don't want to take up your time today to discuss life insurance, but I would like an opportunity to meet with you sometime next week.

Would next Thursday at two-thirty or four be better?"
Why the following week? By suggesting the next week,
he implies that he is very busy, which in turn translates
into the perception that he is successful. Second, it's
easier for the customer to make a commitment to see
him next week. The customer thinks, "I don't have to
deal with it now. I'll cope with it next week," and so
he'll commit himself. But the assumption is the same as
Baker's—a choice of two times is offered, not a question
to be answered with a yes or no.

It's not only in the approach that Baker asks presumptive questions but throughout his entire presentation. Note how the sales experts do it:

- When showing a home, Hardeman assumes the
sale again and again. She'll ask the buyers to picture
in their minds which pieces of their furniture go
where. By saying this, she implies that they have
consented to buy. She gets the same message across
by questioning, "Will you use this room as your little
girl's nursery, or for your upstairs study?"
- "Do you want the premium to be billed to you on
an annual or semiannual basis?" Gandolfo asks. "Do you
want it sent to your office or residence? Do you want
the five-million-dollar or ten-million-dollar policy?"
- "I think if you can buy XYZ Corporation at twenty-
two dollars, it's an excellent value. Should I put you
down for ten thousand or twenty thousand shares at
this price?" Shafiroff tells a prospect.
- "Don't you love the way the blush looks?" Ash
asks a prospect. "Isn't it natural-looking? Doesn't
your face feel so natural and smooth? Don't you
agree that it's just right for your skin?"
- "Do you agree that this proposal covers the applications you had in mind?" Rodgers ask a prospect.
"Do you agree that the cost seems appropriate?"

Throughout the presentation, Hardeman continually
gets her prospects to agree with her, because when

people are nodding their heads in agreement with you, they'll probably feel foolish if, at the end of the conversation, they say no. This is the main reason why it's important to constantly seek agreement by asking questions such as, "Isn't this a nice fireplace?" and "Don't you just love this big bathroom?" You want to get the prospect in the habit of saying yes to everything. In fact, when Hardeman asks a question, before the person can answer, she often says, "Don't you agree?"

When should you first assume the sale? As soon as an appointment for a sales presentation is established. Gandolfo assumes that anyone who agrees to see him must be interested in buying life insurance, so he's automatically going to sell him.

In the case of Mary Kay, each woman is told to bring her checkbook to the beauty class and is told in advance that the class will last two hours. Mary Kay assumes that anyone who attends is doing so because she wants to buy something. If there are going to be six women attending, the consultant will bring six kits—so that everyone can buy one.

Buck Rodgers has a somewhat different view about the sale: "I don't think a salesperson should think that just because an appointment is given to him it's going to result in a sale." He doesn't think you should ever take anyone for granted. Especially when it comes to selling a big-ticket item. In all likelihood, the prospect may be considering four or five other competitive products. So, the fact that you get your foot in the door is not a reason to assume that you'll automatically get the sale.

What Rodgers assumes on the initial call is that somewhere in the prospect's organization there is a problem— some part needs help, guidance, and constructive input. The real secret for him is to be able to separate the real problems from the myriad issues that people focus on but that aren't necessarily the hot points. He never takes anything for granted. He questions and probes until he is able to sense the problem(s) that is the real source of trouble. Then, he jumps on it and attempts to solve the *right* problem. He believes it's important not to get sidetracked and waste a lot of time on unimportant things.

Buck Rodgers sums up his thoughts by adding, "While I feel a salesperson should walk in thinking that every prospect represents a potential sale, he should also understand that sometimes people are going to turn him down. He must be able to accept that rejection comes with the territory. Yet, he can't let rejection become a negative influence. A salesperson must be able to take the no's and keep right on going to the next call with his enthusiasm intact."

Overcoming Objections

It's been said that if it weren't for objections, a salesperson would be nothing more than an order taker. If so, there would be no need for companies to pay nice, fat commission checks. So, while none of us likes objections, we must accept them as part of the business and make sure we know how to overcome them.

There is some controversy among the sales experts on how to interpret objections. Shafiroff believes that objections are simply requests for more information. The prospect isn't really saying no. Instead, he's saying, "I'm not convinced yet. Give me some more reasons to buy."

Gandolfo has another interpretation. He believes the prospect is saying, "I don't trust you." In his opinion, most people won't actually state that in fact they don't trust you, so instead they use objections as smokescreens. In this case, it's the salesperson's job to try to convince the prospect that his best interests are at heart.

Beginning with his telephone approach, Baker encounters resistance. In the prospect's office, Silver emphatically states, "I'm not interested." When Baker makes another attempt to create some interest, he is told a second time, "I said I'm not interested." It's only when he tells Silver the story of how the U. S. Patent Office was nearly abolished because they thought there were no new ideas that Silver finally consents to hear him out.

The patent-office story is often used by Gandolfo, who follows it by adding, "Mr. Prospect, while it may seem corny, let me ask you another question. If you and I went into the pharmacy business, wouldn't we stock our shelves with the most up-to-date drugs for our customers?" When he agrees, Gandolfo continues, "I'm sure you attend seminars and meetings to keep updated on the latest changes in your industry. Likewise, so do I. In my field, new ideas, concepts, and changes in tax laws occur every year. All I want to do is run them by you. If they fit with your philosophy and pocketbook, fine; if not, I promise you I'll be on my way. Certainly you will agree to do this, won't you?" Gandolfo claims that this approach has worked well for him, and it could work for every salesperson, regardless of the product.

Throughout Hardeman's real estate career, she has observed that the prospects who have given her the most initial resistance are ultimately the easiest ones to sell—once she gets them to listen to her. All too often the typical salesperson is frightened away when the so-called tough prospect insists that he or she is not interested. Hardeman has discovered that this type of individual generally has very little resistance to sales-people and knows that if he consents to listen to a sales presentation he has a difficult time saying no to the sale. For this reason, he usually tries to avoid salespeo-ple—and usually succeeds. And, while the salespeople who do get "in" are few and far between, their persis-tence usually pays off.

Shafiroff calls it *telephone pollution*. Today's execu-tives must develop a built-in defense mechanism to protect themselves. They are bombarded with nonpro-fessional solicitation on the telephone and often get it from both ends—as consumers and as businesspeople. There are so many salespeople trying to get through to them on the telephone that it's not possible for them to take the time to listen to every presentation. Yet, they do realize that they can't remain isolated and shut out all salespeople. So, they're selective, but not unreachable. Now, because so few salespeople have the tenacity to get through to them, the difficult prospect hears relatively few sales presentations. With this in mind, Shafiroff maintains that there is a higher-than-usual closing ratio for these presentations that are completed. Many of his major clients gave him a most difficult time when he first approached them. If he had shied away from them, he says, his existing client list would be considerably reduced.

In Mary Kay's business, many times a woman will attend a beauty class but not want to participate. She'll say, "I've been using product X for years and I like it very much."

The response to this is, "I know you're happy with what you're presently using. What I really would like is your opinion about our cosmetics. So I'd appreciate it if you'd try ours and make a comparison between what you presently use and Mary Kay." Initially, Mary Kay consultants never make an attempt to convince any woman that they can make her more beautiful. At this point, no woman would believe it anyhow. The only mission of the consultant is to get everyone involved in the beauty class.

According to Ash, every now and then during a group presentation there's one woman who will be difficult. She will make several derogatory remarks such as, "That's a pretty pink Cadillac parked in front. They must pay you a high commission," or, "Can't you get right to the bottom line and tell us how much this stuff costs?" Generally, all this person really wants is attention, so Ash recommends "giving her a barrel full of it." This is always a better way to handle a harasser than to put him or her down. With compliments and kindness, not only can you eventually win the troublemaker over, but in a group presentation you can win over everyone else too.

Mary Kay says, "There are those times when a woman might make a strong case for the cosmetics she's presently using. 'I've been using brand X for years, and it's simply wonderful,' a customer might say.

"When I hear this," says Mary Kay, "I reply, 'I'm sure it's a fine product, but I don't know a lot about it. I have heard that it's good.' I *never* knock the competition, because it only boosts the other product. I simply acknowledge it, and go on from there."

Like Mary Kay, in *The Perfect Sales Presentation* Baker deals with the competition by complimenting Silver's present clothing source. He says to Silver, "Meyer Brothers is an excellent store."

Rodgers handles a prospect's question, "What makes you think your equipment is superior to XYZ Company?" by responding, "Look, if you want to know something about the other fellow's product, you should talk to him. Now, I will be very specific with you about what our products and our services are like. Then, its up to you to make a comparison."

If he's told that a competitor is also presently under consideration and asked to give an opinion of them, Rodgers replies, "It's a fine company. The key is for you to determine who can give you the greatest value. Who is going to help your bottom line? And when you run into difficulties, who is going to be here to solve your problems? I am. I am the person who is going to provide all of that for you. Through me and my access to all of the resources necessary within my company, we will get your job done."

Gandolfo comments on how Baker ignores Silver's remark ("Hey, I didn't say I was buying today,") in response to being asked to state his height. Wisely, Baker doesn't take a defensive position but instead continues with his presentation as if he didn't hear the statement. "Many times, I, too, am asked why I'm filling out an insurance application, and I simply continue with the next question as if there had been no objection. For instance, somebody might say, 'Hey,

Joe, why are you asking me the questions on that application? I didn't say I wanted to buy a policy.' I'm oblivious to such comments. I just automatically continue with my next question by saying, 'I understand. Now what is your exact height and weight?' I do the same thing sometimes when a prospect says, 'Joe, I want to sleep on it,' or, 'I never do business with a stranger.' I might just nod in agreement and continue with my presentation. Or I might say, 'Yeah, I'm the same way,' and ignore the remark. What a salesperson doesn't want to do is say, 'Why do you feel that way?' If he does, the prospect may feel that he must defend his position. You never want to make anyone have to eat his words."

Baker doesn't make a big deal out of Silver's reaction to his suits costing $475 and $525 rather than $375. Hardeman notes, "He is smart to avoid a long, drawn-out discussion on why wool suits are higher priced than the blends. I think it's a mistake for a salesperson to feel as though he has to justify the higher cost of an obviously better value. For instance, when I take a prospect out to view two homes and one has certain features demonstrating a pronounced difference in price, I let the facts speak for themselves. There are times when it's simply not necessary for a salesperson to say anything. You've got to know when to keep quiet."

Regarding another objection, Baker handles Silver's comment, "I'd like to sleep on it. I'll let you know when I return from L.A.," by creating a sense of urgency. Shafiroff does the same thing if a prospect objects by making such statements as, "I want to think it over"; "I want to talk it over with my spouse"; "This isn't a good time"; etc. Shafiroff thinks it's important to realize that when you hear these kinds of objections, you shouldn't take it personally, because the prospect really isn't rejecting you or your product. He or she is only delaying his decision making. Long ago Shafiroff discovered that most people have difficulty in making decisions that are unrelated to their field of expertise.

For example, surgeons who can make quick life-and-death decisions in the operating room might have difficulty picking out a tie in a haberdashery. The same is true with an executive of a large manufacturing company when it comes to investing in the stock market. Their fear is based on the fact that they're feeling insecure, and consequently they think that by taking no action, a wrong decision will be avoided. They associate decision making with risk taking—and anytime there are risks, there could be trouble. Shafiroff feels that it's the salesperson's job to convince the prospect that being indecisive and doing nothing is a greater mistake than making the wrong decision. This is particularly true in any business where timing is important. Like Baker, Shafiroff creates a sense of urgency by countering objections with a convincing explanation of why it's in the prospect's best interest to act today versus sometime in the future.

In the securities field, a sense of urgency is natural because the price of an investment is subject to daily fluctuations. A delay on the prospect's part could be costly. With this in mind, Shafiroff says, "Mr. Prospect, we both agree that timing is crucial in anything we do, and this is particularly true in the case of an undervalued stock such as this. . . . I believe the time for us to act is now."

Gandolfo has another feeling on this subject. He believes that when prospects procrastinate, it is generally because the salesperson lacks conviction and sincerity. They're telling the salesperson, "You make me feel uncomfortable. You're cold and uncaring." Gandolfo believes this is particularly true when you're confronted with a barrage of objections one after another such as, "I want to think it over"; "I want to talk to my friend who sells insurance"; "I can't afford it right now."

Just the same, there are some strong rebuttals for each of these common objections. When a prospect states that he wants to think it over, Gandolfo's reply is, "May I ask you a question? What other information would you need later that would help you make a decision?" Often, if he lets the prospect talk enough, the customer will talk himself out of his protest altogether.

When told that a friend handles the prospect's insurance needs, Gandolfo replies, "That's interesting, because so many of my clients have expressed to me how difficult it is to go to a friend or relative when a complaint arises. They'd *rather* deal with somebody on strictly a business basis. Then, too, there's a great deal of confidential information that you probably wouldn't want to reveal to a friend or relative."

And when somebody states that he can't afford it, Gandolfo is apt to fire back, "May I ask you a question? Would you kindly explain to me why you consented to see me about discussing life insurance if you can't afford it? Now I'd appreciate it if you would tell me the real reason."

When Rodgers faces an indecisive person, he uses a more direct approach. "Look," he will say, "you have procrastinated and there's no reason why you can't make a decision, because all of the facts are here. Let's just go through everything once more." If Rodgers still faces indecisiveness, he'll conclude, "I've done everything I can to convince you that you should buy. Evidently you're not convinced, so there's no need for us to have additional discussion. I recommend that you think it over, and I'll get back to you in thirty to sixty days. I have given you the best proposition why you should buy, but for some reason you're still not ready to make the decision. There's no sense in my spending any more time with you today. It's not fair to either one of us." Over a period of time, a salesperson knows how far to go without upsetting a prospect when a no is given. That's the point when you should back off. Furthermore, you should never appear to be begging for someone's business. Rodgers gives a future date and suggests that he will be happy to follow up then to see if there's any interest. Then he goes on to a more promising prospect.

Baker's company, Winchester, makes higher-priced
suits than Silver is accustomed to buying. Understandably, this is a barrier to overcome. Objecting to the price
of a product is a common hurdle for salespeople, and
it's interesting to observe how the sales experts handle
it.

With Gandolfo and Shafiroff; selling life insurance
and securities depends upon their arriving at a price
with which the prospect will feel comfortable. For example, if a million-dollar policy is not affordable, perhaps a smaller one will be affordable. Likewise, instead
of recommending ten thousand shares of XYZ Company, Shafiroff will suggest that his prospect take a
smaller position. "I understand why you're not prepared to take a position of ten thousand shares," he will
say, "but you agree that this investment can benefit you
substantially. And you agree with me that timing is the
key consideration. So, instead of making the maximum
investment now, which I know you would make if you
had the available funds today, let's take advantage of
the timing of this extraordinary value with a minimum
commitment. I suggest five thousand shares." If Shafiroff
senses hesitation, he comes back with a smaller amount;
Or would you feel more comfortable with three thousand shares?"

When a woman mentions that her husband might
object to her spending too much money at a beauty
class, Ash replies, "We women know that when we
want something special, and it's simply not in the budget, we know how to do great and terrific things with
hamburger and chicken to take a little out of the gro-
cery allowance. When we have to, we can cut a corner
here and there to get some of those things that we
really want." She simplifies it further by adding, "When
you break it down, the cost of six months' worth of
skin-care products and cosmetics is only about the cost
of one soft drink per day. Certainly you can afford that
or something so important as your skin."

Although he sells a considerably higher-priced prod-

uct, Rodgers, too, talks budget, but on a much large
scale, when presenting a computer system. When some
body states that Rodgers's product is too expensive, hi
reply is, "Have you looked at what we are able t
provide you in the way of total savings? Rather tha
looking at the cost on a monthly, semiannual, or yearl
basis, because you are in business for a long time, hav
you considered what this means to you over the nex
five years? When you allocate your cost over a long-tern
cycle, you'll see that this equipment represents a sub
stantial savings as compared to the way you're present
doing things. Furthermore, here's how we have docu
mented both the tangible and intangible savings tha
we believe can be realized by your company." Accord
ing to Rodgers, it's merely a matter of demonstratin,
the cost justification in black and white.

When one of Hardeman's prospects objects to th
price of a home, she simply states, "I know the market
and I don't think there's anything better in this pric
range. For the money, this is the best value in thi
area." If the prospect still grumbles, she says, "Perhap
you should go up another ten thousand dollars or so an
buy more house. Or I can show you other homes in
different neighborhood that will give you more for you
money, but the community isn't as nice."

When Hardeman believes a prospect likes a hous
but continues to object to one or two things about it
she adds, "There isn't a perfect house out there. N
matter which house you buy, there are probably goin,
to be one or two things that you would like changed
And even if you had built the house, before the con
struction was completed, you would change your min
about a few things."

However, Hardeman concludes, "If they have to
many objections, I keep showing properties until w
find the right home that makes them happy. And if w
can't find one, we can build it for them, which take
approximately four to six months."

Closing
the Sale

"There's no magic to closing the sale. It's the highlight of a sales presentation," Rodgers states. "Right from the initial approach to the very end, bit by bit, the salesperson is closing the sale. It's when you find out if you did your job properly."

"It's the moment of truth," Shafiroff emphasizes.

"I just go with my instincts and close whenever they tell me to," Hardeman says.

"Closing is the most natural thing about selling," Ash says.

"It's no big deal," Gandolfo says. "Closing the sale is automatic."

This is what the five sales experts have to say about closing the sale. Yet, when asked the same question, the majority of salespeople hem and haw and give complicated, drawn-out explanations, *And that's exactly what they do when they attempt to close a sale!* They hesitate to ask for an order. They talk too much. They oversell. Consequently, prospects become indecisive and resistant. It's the old monkey-see, monkey-do principle.

"You've got to have complete confidence in your ability to close the sale," Gandolfo stresses. "If not, the prospect becomes consumed with doubt. He knows when it's time for you to close the sale, and it's up to you to ask for the order. He knew what you were there for when he agreed to see you, and if you lack confidence to ask for his business, he's going to lack confidence in making a decision."

To Rodgers, closing the sale is simply "demonstrating a confidence that you're ready to provide the prospect with the service that he wants," Rodgers explains. "When the prospect feels comfortable with you in this regard, it's time to say, 'Okay, let's sign the order.' "

Either way, it's contagious, Shafiroff believes. "When you confidently ask for the order, the other person becomes confident too. It's a natural reaction, and the prospect feels he's doing the right thing. He thinks it's a mistake not to act. It's only when a salesperson is full of doubt himself that people hesitate and feel as though they're being put under the gun to make a decision. Hesitation is every bit as contagious as confidence."

Baker's sales presentation has a nice, rhythmic flow, and his close naturally blends in with his proposal so that the prospect is unaware of a precise moment when he can think, "Ah, now he's putting the squeeze on me to buy."

Mary Kay thinks pressure selling is outdated. "Women, especially, are resentful of anyone who tries to stuff something down their throats. And they resist it."

When Silver states that he'd "like to sleep on it" and will make his buying decision upon returning from L.A., Baker creates a sense of urgency. He explains the possible shortage of inventory that is likely to occur by delaying the buying decision—the prospect has something to lose. In fact, this creating-a-sense-of-urgency technique is a "natural" that works with almost any product. Following are examples of how each of the five sales experts does it.

Shafiroff believes a good sales presentation always creates a sense of urgency. In the securities field, it's simply a matter of pointing out to the prospect that the price of a particular stock may rise in the next few days. When he believes this, he might tell a client, "The time to make this investment is now. It's important that we accumulate these shares at twelve or less. At this price the shares are selling below four times earnings. That's extraordinary for a company with such an outstanding record. Let's take advantage of the opportunity. I suggest taking a position of ten thousand shares at this price." Then, after a brief pause, he says, "Do you feel comfortable with that?"

When selling a life insurance policy, it's a matter of pointing out to the prospect that his health may change and he will no longer be insurable. According to Gandolfo, a delay might mean that the prospect can't qualify tomorrow or next week. "None of us has a crystal ball and can see into the future. If you were to die before you qualify for this policy, your family would be destitute."

A Mary Kay consultant takes enough complete sets to every beauty show so that each prospect can take home everything she wants that *same* day. "Women can be impetuous, and what they want, they want right now! They don't want to wait six weeks until something ordered in a catalog arrives," Ash states. Mary Kay consultants try to create enough need so that the prospect wants to begin applying good skin care immediately. While the proper use of the product is still fresh in the prospect's mind, the consultant convinces her that *now is the time to act*. Years ago, Mary Kay worked for a direct sales company that delivered the merchandise four weeks after the presentation. By the time the product was delivered, her customers didn't even remember the instructions on how to use what they had bought. In many cases they didn't even remember ordering it!

Hardeman states that a home is a one-of-a-kind item. "I tell my clients, 'In Atlanta, where we have multiple listings, every real estate agent in town can sell a listed property. And there are more than several thousand agents in town.' So, if a prospect waits too long, somebody else might purchase the home the prospect wants.

Now, I am hesitant to tell a prospect this, because I never want to appear as if I'm pressuring anyone to buy a home. So, unless I feel that the individuals really trust me, I don't mention this to them—however, it happens to be true with every home. When I do say it, I cushion it by adding, 'You know, it's possible that this home might not sell for a year, but on the other hand, you never know when it might go. If you really feel this is the home you want, you should go ahead and put a contract on it.' " Then, too, because the money market fluctuates, when rates are attractive, Hardeman sometimes mentions that clients should try to get a loan commitment while good financing is still available. Finally, she sometimes advises her clients that the prices of homes traditionally rise in the spring, pointing out that (depending on the season, of course) now might be the best time to buy.

Rodgers feels that when a computer system is properly presented to a prospective customer, it becomes obvious that the prospect's problem can be solved. Therefore, there's a built-in urgency to go ahead and write up the order to have it installed. It's a matter of demonstrating that his proposal is so cost justified from the customer's point of view that, as a prudent businessperson, he or she readily recognizes the value Rodgers's company offers. When a salesperson accomplishes this, the prospect is ready to sign.

Baker effectively uses the minor-major close, a selling technique employed in almost all fields. The premise of this close is to avoid asking a prospect to make a *major* buying decision. Instead, he asks a series of relatively minor questions to which the prospect can easily answer yes. The theory is that it is easier to make several minor decisions than one major one. For example, had Baker not used this technique, the prospect could have been asked to make the major decision: "Do you want to buy two suits for $1,134.20?"

Instead, Baker asks "easy" questions that require little thought to answer, such as:

- Should I put down a vest for each suit?
- Do you want to pay by credit card or check?
- You may pay half now and the balance on delivery or the full amount now. Which do you prefer?

Likewise, Gandolfo asks the same kind of questions:

- Should we put down your wife as beneficiary?
- Do you want the waiver of premium?
- Do you want to pay on an annual basis?
- Are you interested in the accidental-death benefit?
- I recommend the automatic premium loan. Is this okay with you?
- Do you want the premiums sent to your home or your business?
- Is $500,000 enough coverage to apply for at this time?
- Is next Tuesday a good time for you to have your physical examination?
- Here are the names and addresses of doctors in your area. Look at this list and tell me which physician would be most convenient for you to see.

None of Gandolfo's questions is hard to answer. On the other hand, imagine the difficulty a prospect would have when asked, "Do you want to buy five hundred thousand dollars of life insurance today for nine thousand dollars?" If so, Gandolfo would have to ask for a check for that amount. Most people would have trouble saying yes to a closing question like that.

As previously explained, most people simply don't like to make major decisions. They don't want to risk making a mistake, so they tend to procrastinate—particularly when the decision involves money. However, it's not difficult to make up one's mind about things that are relatively insignificant. This is precisely what Baker does with Silver. He presents small decisions for Silver to make—each one in itself is painless and requires no effort. But, by agreeing again and again, the prospect is making a major decision.

While the minor-major close is one of the most popular closing techniques in selling, another sales strategy, especially effective when selling expensive products, is the approach that Rodgers uses in asking for an order. What has worked best for him over the years is to say, "Look, we've spent a lot of time together, and I clearly understand your problem. I think I have the best answer, so let's you and I proceed and we'll get the equipment in as soon as possible." If there's any hesitation, he adds, "Let's get the order signed and then we'll take the next step." Some salespeople lead the prospect into a buying decision by taking him through a series of step-by-step minor decisions, but in Rodgers's opinion, nothing beats being direct and simply asking for the order.

Although Silver suggests that Baker call back, Baker closes the sale on the spot. He prefers to go "double or nothing," figuring that the odds are in his favor if he closes the sale while the prospect is still "hot."

According to Ash, some people "just cool off." The best time for them to make buying decisions is while all of the facts are fresh in their minds, and that's immediately after the product has been presented. She thinks that the more time expires, the less people's memories retain what you've told them. They can't remember the reasons why they need the product and, in the case of beauty care, how to use it. But they do remember how much it costs. With each day that passes, they remember less and less about the product, and simultaneously the price seems proportionately higher for the benefits they think they get. For this reason, only a relatively small percentage of callbacks are closed by salespeople.

Gandolfo is a "percentage player." When a person tells him, "I want to think it over. Will you call me back in a few days?" Gandolfo replies, "I'm sorry, but I can't." No matter how sincere someone may be in making this request, Gandolfo always gives the same answer. In most instances, people accept it and he automatically continues to close the sale by asking for the order. On occasion, however, someone will ask, "Why can't you call me back?" To this, Gandolfo says, "Because I don't operate like that. I would be doing you a disservice if I allowed you to procrastinate. The best time for you to make your decision is right *now*, while all of the facts are fresh in your mind. And if there is something that you don't understand, I'm right here to answer it for you." With that, he listens carefully to any objection that may be voiced, then continues to ask for the order.

Gandolfo is convinced that the longer a person has to think it over, the lower the odds become to make the sale. Believing this, he goes with the percentages and attempts to close the sale while he's eyeball to eyeball with the prospect. While now and then he might lose a sale with this approach, in the long run he's far ahead.

According to Rodgers, a salesperson begins closing the sale bit by bit, throughout the presentation. Relatively early in the presentation, Baker lets Silver know that Baker is expecting a decision to be made at the close of his presentation. He accomplishes this by saying, "I deal with successful people who have the self-confidence to make decisions. Selecting a wardrobe is a minor decision in comparison to the major ones you must make every day. I like dealing with men like you who have the ability to act—and don't procrastinate. Fortunately, I don't deal with Mr. Milquetoasts. That would bother me." Of course, the real message behind this powerful statement is: *I expect you to make a buying decision today!*

Early in Gandolfo's career he lost a lot of sales because prospects would say at the end of the presentation, "I want to talk it over with my spouse."

He heard this objection so often that he finally figured out how to overcome it. Before he set up a date for an appointment, he would say, "Now, is it necessary for your wife [or husband] to be present in order for you to make a decision?" If the prospect said yes, he then would schedule the appointment at a convenient time to talk to both of them. Also, when he calls on businesspeople, he uses the same approach: "Whoever is necessary to make a buying decision should be present." Sometimes it's a partner, company officer, attorney, accountant, or comptroller. Because he has prepared them in advance, he is rarely told at the end of his presentation, "I want to talk it over with my . . ."

Shafiroff unequivocally believes that the close is the most important part of any sales presentation (which consists of three parts: an introduction, a body, and a close). He states that the majority of salespeople, however, get so bogged down during their approach and explanation of their product that they fail to spend enough time closing the sale. According to Shafiroff, a typical telephone presentation in the securities industry lasts approximately twenty minutes, with the introduction taking four minutes and the reasons for buying occupying fourteen minutes. That leaves only two minutes for the close! So Shafiroff turns things around. He allows two minutes for his introduction (note that he has already spoken to the prospect once before and sent out a follow-up letter); the explanation of his product lasts four to six minutes; this leaves fourteen to sixteen minutes for him to ask for the order. With this structure, if he doesn't give a complete explanation in four to six minutes, he can do so with the remaining time when he answers objections. His rebuttals to objections are an integral part of his presentation because it's not necessary to overwhelm the prospect with too much technical information. There's no need to oversell to the point where you feel you must prove how much you know about your business. Besides, the average busy person becomes impatient after fifteen or twenty minutes on the telephone—perhaps even sooner.

In addition, Shafiroff asks for the order three times.

After he answers each objection, he attempts to close the sale once more. "Fine, Mr. Prospect, I understand that. Now you agree with me that timing is critical?" Based on his personal experiences, Shafiroff believes that salespeople who attempt to close three times instead of one increase their productivity fivefold. With those odds, he thinks that it makes a lot of sense to ask a second and third time. Beyond the third request, the law of diminishing returns sets in, and the closing ratio begins to decrease with each additional attempt.

There are times when certain objections are good buying signals. In Hardeman's case, when prospects say such things as "Except for the small family room . . ." or "It needs a good paint job," they're actually expressing their interest in making a purchase. As a salesperson, you must listen carefully and not throw in the towel each time somebody voices an objection or directly says no.

It's no secret why you're there. And it's no secret why your prospect is listening. He knows you're there for a purpose, and it's in the best interests of both parties to reach a favorable agreement on that purpose. With this in mind, everyone benefits when the sale is closed.

Servicing
the Customer

In our highly competitive free-enterprise society, a situation rarely exists where one product is far superior to all others in the marketplace. It doesn't matter what you are selling—automobiles, clothing, computers, insurance, real estate, securities—if you don't provide outstanding service, your competition will get the business. In today's market, a great product, without service, isn't enough.

Sadly, however, there are many companies that put too much emphasis on their selling efforts at the expense of providing good service. Some of this attitude stems perhaps from our being so results-driven that a disproportionate amount of time and money are invested in generating record-breaking sales volume year after year. Unfortunately, it's done at the expense of taking care of those customers already on the books! Such neglect is very shortsighted. The most successful organizations and salespersons provide their customers with outstanding service. Selling and servicing must go hand in hand.

IBM is known for its service, which is based on three principles: the individual is always respected; the customer will receive the best possible service in the world; excellence is the goal in every activity.

What many salespeople fail to realize is that once the sale is closed, that's only the beginning. At IBM an order is never considered complete until a system is successfully installed. The two words *sell-install* go together; you can't have one without the other. This is why IBM's marketing people are told that getting the order may be the easiest step in the process. The sale doesn't end there. They are told that "nothing is sold until it's properly installed; nothing is ever installed until it's properly sold." The delivery-and-installation phase of a sale might take as long as a year. During this time, they must educate the customer and demonstrate how to apply the product properly. Also, they work constantly with customers to try to find new applications to further justify the equipment.

To Shafiroff's way of thinking, an account doesn't become a client until repeated transactions have built what he considers a lasting relationship.

Hardeman sees her business as service-driven, as she feels service is the key to the real estate business. The only things she has to sell are service and knowledge. Her feeling is that there are a lot of agents who know the business as well as she does. She believes in giving her customers so much service that they will feel guilty even thinking about doing business with anybody else.

Repeat business is the name of the game for all leading salespeople. Gandolfo feels that after a two-year period, eighty percent of a service-oriented salesperson's sales volume should be generated either from repeat business or from referrals by satisfied clients.

It's a continual building process, and a good salesperson builds a solid base with his existing clientele because he services them. Those salespeople who don't take care of their clients are shortsighted and, in the long run, end up on the short end of the stick. Year after year they pound the pavement, always seeking new business, without the benefit of having built a solid base of satisfied clients. In the real estate field, not only does Hardeman get repeat business by homes turning over every few years, but she's constantly having people referred to her. For instance, she points out that once a client recommended eight of his friends to her—all of whom bought or sold homes through her.

Baker also services Silver's future clothing needs. This is his edge over the competition, since he isn't the only clothing source in town. Even though his prices are slightly higher than what Silver is currently paying, like many businesspeople, Silver is willing to pay extra money for good service.

The fact is that the most successful salespersons and marketing organizations rank highest in retention of business. It is believed that the amount of referred business and repeat orders is directly proportionate to the quality and amount of service rendered.

Too many salespersons are so eager to generate new business that they neglect to follow up on the orders they do get, Shafiroff believes. In telephone selling, he begins the follow-up process immediately after the sale is closed—*before he puts the receiver down*. In the securities field, he's witnessed brokers who are evidently so filled with anxiety that as soon as the customer places an order they say, "I put you down for two thousand shares at fifty dollars. Thank you and goodbye." Then, as soon as they hang up, they're on the phone with another prospect. They fail to make adequate notes of their transactions, and by the end of the day they can't remember who bought what. No wonder there are so many mix-ups with their orders. Then, they blame it on the computer! To open a new account in Shafiroff's field, certain information about the customer is mandatory. What he does is repeat the details of the transaction back to the client, express his gratitude for the business, and put an assistant on the phone to ask the questions that his company requires. Then, like Baker, he immediately sends a follow-up letter. In addition to thanking the customer for his business, he encloses some literature about the investment, including the latest annual report, a quarterly statement, his firm's written recommendation on it, and some financial information about his brokerage house. Also, again like Baker, he jots down notes on a three-by-five card about his conversation with the client. Included are such things as his impression of him, his comments about his existing portfolio, and the date when he should next contact him. The card is placed in a chronological file, and, like clockwork, he makes sure to call him at the appropriate time. As time passes, additional information is added to the client's card: special interests, hobbies, facts about family, and so on.

Gandolfo also sends a thank-you letter. Although it seems like such a small thing, people really appreciate it. On the rare occasions when any of us receives a letter of this nature, we think, "This guy really cares about me. I'm glad I'm doing business with him."

Many people are suspicious of salesmen. They think that a salesman is there at the time of the sale but not when you need him if something goes wrong. Many people get "buyer's remorse." Soon after the sale they think, "Did I make the right decision? Maybe I shouldn't have spent so much money." But when they get that follow-up letter, it makes them think, "Yes. I did the right thing."

Mary Kay consultants automatically follow up with each customer, too. At the end of the beauty class the consultant talks to each woman privately and schedules an appointment to do a checkup facial. If one isn't booked, she'll call the woman in two weeks and say, "I just want to know how you're doing with your cosmetics." With a copy of the customer's order in front of her, she says, "How is your basic set working for you? Do you see any improvement in your skin?" She'll ask a series of positive questions; most important, the consultant wants to find out if anything is wrong.

For instance, the customer might say, "Well, I'm not too happy with the rouge. It's the wrong color." The consultant will ask if she can come by so that she can give the customer an exchange.

In most cases, the consultant will exchange it, even if it means taking a loss. And, in those few instances where a customer is unhappy, the company will give her a full refund, which is part of their 100-percent-money-back guarantee. They don't want anyone to be dissatisfied with their products. They believe that when there is a problem, by having an opportunity to see the customer, there's a good chance to solve it.

Baker calls Silver to let him know that a problem exists with the order. Shafiroff also believes in promptly and regularly relaying any bad news. He thinks that too many salespeople call only when they have something good to report. In the securities field, many brokers are good about informing their clients about a rise in the price of an investment. They'll also notify their clients about a declared stock dividend, or a stock split, or an announced increase in earnings. But they tend to shy away from relaying bad news about such things as a poor earnings report, a cut in dividends, or a sharp drop in price. Shafiroff believes you must communicate the disappointments as well as the good news. He has found that his clients appreciate his concern about their investments, and, by contacting them, he rarely loses their business. It's the salesperson who fails to communicate the bad news whom customers are most likely to abandon.

Rodgers believes that you also must stay in touch with your customers when things are going well. You don't neglect your customer and come around only when it's time to put out a fire. The Johnny-come-lately salesperson has no rapport with his customer and fails to demonstrate that he truly cares about his welfare *before* the problem arises. It doesn't work to arrive after the fact and be faced with an irate customer who says, "Where were you before we had this problem?" For this reason, he recommends seeing customers every so often when things are going smoothly and saying, "I just stopped in to make sure everything is going well. What can I do for you?" When you do this customers think, "Now here's a salesperson who really has my interest at heart."

Hardeman believes that constant communication is the key to building a lasting relationship with customers. This is particularly true when a seller lists his house with her. Nothing disenchants homeowners more than the real estate agent who fails to inform them of what's happening with his listing. Generally, what causes grief is not that the agent isn't doing his work properly but that he has left the seller out in left field.

It's inexcusable when a client has to call the salesperson to find out about the status of his house. You must stay in touch. For instance, before Hardeman places an ad in the newspaper, she'll call and say, "I just wrote this ad on your home. Let me read it to you"; "I showed the home to two couples today, but there wasn't any interest. I have three showings scheduled later this week"; "I suggest that you leave on the end table lights in the living room"; "On Wednesday I'm planning on having a luncheon in your house and will have some other agents come over to view it"; "I had a flyer made up that I am keeping in the house for other agents"; "On Monday I'm having a photographer take some pictures of your home."

The secret is to stay in constant contact with the seller. There are so many things a good agent does to sell a home, but unless the seller is told about them, he never knows. And when the agent does all of these things but keeps it a secret, after the house is finally sold the seller thinks the agent didn't work hard enough to earn his commission Or, even worse, when the listing expires, the seller is so frustrated that he gives it to another agent. By keeping in touch with the seller, not only does he think you've earned your pay, but he's delighted to refer you to his friends and relatives.

"There are dozens of little things to do for the buyer *after* the sale," according to Hardeman. For starters, she's constantly updating the buyer on the status of the loan. In the case of out-of-towners, she'll make sure that their utilities are turned on. If a deposit is required because the previous owner turned them off, she'll even make a deposit. She'll meet the movers at the home when the owners can't be there. She'll get them information on the schools and community activities that she thinks will interest the family. She'll recommend doctors in the area. When she knows several people in the community, she'll invite neighbors to join her with the new homeowners for lunch. She always gives a nice housewarming gift to every buyer. In the past, her gifts have included expensive plants, fine pieces of crystal, and recently she's been giving beautiful drawings of the home. With as many as sixty listings at any given time, she has a full-time secretary to handle most of these details for her. But to Hardeman, the important thing is to make sure her clients receive this service.

Even though IBM is a $50 billion corporation today, the company has striven to maintain what Rodgers refers to as a "lightness of foot." He stresses that the company has worked very hard over the years to project a well-deserved image that states: *We're responsive.* Rodgers refers to IBM's practice of responding within twenty-four hours to any customer complaint, anywhere in the world. If they can't respond in person they do it by phone, by letter, or by wire. While not implying that every problem will be solved within twenty-four hours, the customer at least knows that the company is aware of the troubles. The customer hears, "We're listening, and something will be done to solve your problem."

Even in the case of a sale that involves an expensive computer system, Rodgers concurs that it's not enough to do the major things well, it's doing the little things that often makes the difference. He is a stickler on details, an important facet of servicing the customer that he feels many salespeople overlook. For example, he promptly returns all telephone calls to customers. If he's running late for an appointment, he'll make a quick call to let the customer know that an unavoidable delay has occurred. If he's on the road or out of the country, his secretary automatically acknowledges the caller's inquiry and informs him or her that Rodgers will be in touch upon his return. He doesn't give anyone an excuse to complain. If a salesperson says he's going to drop off a brochure or a proposal and then fails to do it promptly, he risks nullifying any good will that may have been created. Giving immediate attention lets the customer know that you're dependable, and when something major occurs, you respond at once.

Whenever Rodgers makes a call in the field, upon his return to his office he routinely follows up with a letter thanking the customer for the meeting and for their business relationship. He also summarizes the discussion and reviews their action plan with the company. Then, at the appropriate time, days or weeks later, he makes a follow-up telephone call to the customer to make sure the customer is satisfied with the results.

Shafiroff emphasizes that once he opens a new account, no matter what size the initial order is, it represents only the beginning. Baker is well aware that Silver's two-suit order is only the "tip of the iceberg" and that if all goes well his new client will purchase many additional suits over the years, and Shafiroff feels the same way about his new clients. Frequently, small accounts grow into large accounts, by nurturing them with follow-up and good service. Often the initial order is just a "token" one compared to the future business it represents once the salesperson has proven himself or herself. Some of Shafiroff's major accounts resulted from small transactions.

All sales experts strongly believe that outstanding service is mandatory in today's selling world. Yet, while the importance of this is so obvious, sadly only a small percentage of salespeople are ready and willing to provide it. To the mass army of salespeople, "the customer always comes first" is a tired cliché, but to the most successful salespeople it represents a code to live by. To them, making a sale and failing to follow up with the best possible service is tantamount to delivering damaged goods. The customer is cheated because he doesn't receive the true value that's due him for his money. It's a matter of integrity. Every time a sale is made, a salesperson's honor is on the line. No sale is ever completed without providing the service that must accompany it.

PART V
PROFILES OF THE
SALES EXPERTS

Mary Kay Ash

Chairman of the Board
Mary Kay Cosmetics, Inc.

Mary Kay Ash is the founder and chairman of the board of Mary Kay Cosmetics, Inc., a Dallas-based company. In 1963, after representing several direct-selling companies for twenty-five years, she started the company in a five-hundred-square-foot storefront with her son, Richard Rogers, on an initial investment of five thousand dollars. Today, the New York Stock Exchange company has an estimated 150,000 independent beauty consultants located throughout the United States, Canada, Australia, Argentina, and the United Kingdom. It is one of the world's largest direct-selling organizations.

Considered one of America's most admired and dynamic businesswomen, Ash has appeared on many national television shows, including *60 Minutes, Today, Good Morning, America, PM Magazine,* and *The Phil Donahue Show.* She has been featured in numerous magazine articles and has authored two best-selling books: *Mary Kay,* and *Mary Kay on People Management.*

Joe Gandolfo, Ph.D., ChFC, CLU

Life Insurance Agent

For the past ten years, Joe Gandolfo has approached the billion-dollar figure, averaging hundreds of millions per year in life insurance sales. His personal sales production is greater than the majority of life insurance companies. He is considered the number one salesperson in the life insurance field.

Gandolfo holds the CLU designation as a member of the American College of Life Underwriters and is also a Chartered Financial Counselor. He attended Kentucky Military Institute, Vanderbilt University, Miami University of Ohio, and the California Coast University. He holds a master's degree and a Ph.D. in business administration, and he is a life and qualifying member of the Million Dollar Round Table.

He is the author of four books: *Ideas Are a Dime a Dozen; On to a Hundred Million; Selling Is 98% Understanding Human Beings . . . 2% Product Knowledge; God, I'll Give You All the Credit . . . And I'll Take All the Commissions;* and coauthor of *How to Make Big Money Selling*. He has produced several recordings, including his best-selling album *Pay Zero Taxes*. A much sought-after speaker, he has lectured in every state of the Union as well as internationally on estate planning and tax shelters. His clients include several thousand multimillionaires.

Bettye C. Hardeman

Real Estate Agent

Bettye C. Hardeman is considered to be America's top real estate agent selling residential properties.

Since 1968, when she entered the real estate business, Hardeman has been associated with Northside Realty Associates, Inc., in Atlanta, Georgia.

She has been a member of the Million Dollar Club for the past thirteen years, and in 1981 was a recipient of the Phoenix Award, the Atlanta Board of Realtors' most distinguished citation.

During the past four years her sales volume in homes listed and sold was: in 1985, $26.2 million; in 1984, $23.8 million; in 1983, $24.5 million; in 1982, $20.7 million; averaging more than 200 homes per year.

Francis G. ("Buck") Rodgers

Marketing Consultant—IBM

After working for International Business Machines Corporation for thirty-four years, in July 1984, Buck Rodgers elected to take early retirement and presently serves as a consultant to the company. Rodgers has held several marketing and executive positions at IBM and was named president of the Data Processing Division in October 1967. Three years later he was appointed director of marketing, and in June 1974 was named vice-president of marketing, a position he held until his retirement.

Rodgers has received honorary degrees from Miami University (Oxford, Ohio), Hartwick College (Oneonta, New York), and Mount Union College (Alliance, Ohio). He is a member of the Business Advisory Council of Miami University, a member of the Advisory Council of the University of Tennessee, and a member of the Advisory Council of Purdue University. He is a director of Arkwright-Boston Insurance Company, Bergen Brunswig Corporation, and Emery Worldwide. He has served as a trustee of the Marketing Science Institute at Harvard University and is a Woodrow Wilson Visiting Fellow, director of the Sales Executive Club of New York, and a member of the United Nations/Industry Cooperative Programme.

Rodgers is the author of *The IBM Way: Insights into the World's Most Successful Marketing Organization*. He is featured in *Ten Greatest Salespersons* and is widely quoted in the book *In Search of Excellence*. He spends a great deal of time lecturing on college campuses and addressing civic and business organizations and is one of America's most sought-after speakers.

Martin D. Shafiroff

Financial Consultant

Martin D. Shafiroff is a managing director of the investment banking firm of Shearson Lehman/American Express. Shafiroff is believed to be America's leading investment broker, dealing primarily with individuals and wealthy families. In 1984, his business approximated eleven million dollars in commissions, and the market value of his securities transactions approached the billion-dollar mark. These results are the expression of an investment strategy for his clients that requires precise valuation techniques and intensive updating.

Shafiroff became part of the securities industry in 1966, when he joined Eastman Dillon Union Securities. In 1969, he associated himself with Lehman Brothers, and became a managing director in 1977. In 1984, Lehman was acquired by Shearson/American Express. Shafiroff has been the subject of several feature articles in periodicals such as the *Wall Street Journal* and the *Institutional Investor* and is featured in the best-selling book *Ten Greatest Salespersons*. In addition, he is co-author of *Successful Telephone Selling in the '80s*.

PART VI
QUESTIONS AND ANSWERS ABOUT THE PERFECT SALES PRESENTATION

Why was the Michael Baker presentation to Bill Silver chosen for the book?

Because salespeople in all fields can identify with the product sold in *The Perfect Sales Presentation*. First, salespeople selling both intangible and tangible products can relate to Baker's presentation. It's intangible selling because the prospect never actually sees the actual suit (he only sees swatches). Yet, a suit *is* a tangible product. Second, since the sale is made to a businessman, who is also the consumer, both business-oriented and consumer-oriented salespeople can identify with Baker's presentation. His presentation could be given either in a prospect's home or in his office. Third, since every reader has purchased a suit at one time or another, he or she can readily appreciate a professional way to sell one. Finally, *The Perfect Sales Presentation* is an excellent example of concept selling.

What is concept selling?

Concept selling occurs when an idea is sold—rather than the actual product. For instance, Baker sells concepts such as convenience, selection, and service. A

computer salesperson doesn't sell little black boxes but
what those little black boxes will *do*. Likewise, an in
surance agent doesn't sell insurance contracts, he sell
peace of mind, security, and solutions to financial prob
lems resulting from the death of the insured, and soon

What is the proper way for Baker to dress?

Obviously, because Baker sells tailor-made men's suits
he should wear one—in his particular case, a Winches
ter suit. However, dressing in a fine suit is not limite
to clothing salespersons. The important factor in deter
mining a salesperson's wardrobe is the clientele to whom
he caters. For example, a salesperson selling accounting
services to bankers, attorneys, and business executive
should wear conservative suits. However, a less-forma
dress code is appropriate when selling the same prod
uct to farmers and ranchers. Local customs in variou
parts of the country also influence a salesperson's dress
A salesperson calling on businesspersons in Manhatta
will dress differently from one whose territory is rura
Oklahoma.

How does Baker get himself mentally prepared befor the sale?

He believes that every sales presentation will resul
in an order. Although Baker realizes that "nobody sell
'em all," he always approaches each prospect with
positive attitude. "When you walk in thinking that yo
won't get a sale," he insists, "you'll probably be right.
Being properly prepared is the key element that gener
ates self-confidence. Knowing your business backward
and forward is the best confidence builder—it gives yo
self-esteem and, at the same time, demands respec
from others.

Why did Baker address the prospect as "Bill" rathe than "Mr. Silver"?

It's his personal preference to be less formal, and secondly he doesn't want to position himself in a manner that the prospect could interpret as subservient. Every salesperson should address prospects on a first-name basis. And it's not necessary to ask for permission to do so! How do you do it? Simply by calling each prospect by his or her first name.

In reading *The Perfect Sales Presentation*, Baker appears to be enthusiastic. Does it show in his voice, facial expressions, and body language?

Yes. And it's contagious!

Does his conviction also come through?

Yes. He believes in his product and his company. He knows that the customer will receive value, and this conviction is very apparent. Without conviction, a salesperson comes across as insincere and will create doubt and hesitation—thereby destroying the prospect's ability to make a buying decision.

Is it better to confirm an appointment for a sales presentation with a letter or a phone call?

A letter is usually preferable. First, it presents an opportunity to enclose some literature about the salesperson and his company, allowing him to subtly "toot his own horn." Second, confirming the appointment by telephone can give the prospect an out. In Baker's case, it's too convenient for Silver to tell his secretary to say that he's unavailable and could lead to a "don't-you-call-us-we'll-call-you" situation.

Please give advice on what a salesperson should do if a prospect who is obviously in the middle of a project says, "Show me your line. I can do two things at the same time. . . ."

It's important to set the stage for your presentation under the best possible conditions. Without having the prospect's undivided attention, you will operate under a severe handicap. When a receptive prospect requests that you present your product under less-than-ideal conditions, simply reply, "I'm sorry, but I only stopped by to introduce myself and schedule a future meeting. Would next Wednesday at ten be good for you? Or would two on Thursday be more convenient?" You might also explain how important it is for you to have his uninterrupted attention. You must be the one who establishes the time and place—so you always maintain control of the sale.

Baker drops several names of clients throughout the presentation. Please elaborate on why he does this rather than hand a list of customers to the prospect to review.

It's more subtle to casually drop names than to display a long client's list. And, by doing it this way, Baker can control who he wants the prospect to know is a client. Some clients might not serve as centers of influence, and still others don't want their names to be used. Perhaps Silver might resent the fact that his name might someday appear on the list. Also, it's less obvious to casually drop names than to use a long list. A VIP like Silver might be offended if his interpretation of the list was to influence him to buy. It's tantamount to suggesting, "These people deal with us, and they're smart. So, if you're smart, you'll do business with us too." (Although naming clients does accomplish this purpose, it's not so obvious!) Again, the secret to successful name-dropping is being subtle about it.

Although Baker is an expert in his field, he rarely uses technical terms. Some salespersons are very good about letting everyone know how smart they are—why does Baker make everything seem so uncomplicated?

He has enough self-confidence not to feel the need to impress his prospect with his knowledge about the clothing industry. Few prospects are really interested in the technical areas of your business, so don't bore them with complicated and unnecessary details. You may confuse them—and confused people have difficulty in making buying decisions! Of course, when they ask for specific information, you should give it to them.

Are there any circumstances when it's fair play to knock the competition?

Never! If you can't say something good about your competition, don't say anything. If you badmouth them, it will only come back to haunt you—you'll lose your client's respect.

Wasn't Baker's fact-finding session a bit long? He asked too many questions.

No. In addition to being an important part of the sales presentation, the fact-finding session illustrates your sincerity in having a genuine interest in the prospect's welfare.

Is it necessary to really probe a prospect in order to conduct an effective fact-finding session?

With some prospects, you have to. Your "suggestions" feed them with ideas so they can provide the necessary information you seek.

Baker appears to be a good listener. Please comment.

Listening is a vital part of selling. Had Baker failed to listen, he would not have known his prospect's needs and tastes. With more than four thousand different suits to sell, without listening he'd be working in the dark when the time came to show his merchandise.

Why did Baker wait so long before showing swatches?

Because he first had to learn more about his prospect's needs.

How important is it to get the prospect into the act?

It's vital to let him participate. First, it will keep his interest and undivided attention. Second, it is an effective way to control the sale. Third, it's a better way to learn. For example, you can learn only so much about how to play golf by reading and by watching the pro swing the club. . . .

Each time Baker showed a new series of suits, he showed only five swatches at a time. Why did he limit the selection to five?

Too many choices confuse the buyer and cause decision-making difficulties. Five is the maximum number to present to a prospect—regardless of the product. In fact, some sales experts think the perfect number is three. When three items are offered, it's estimated that fifty percent of the people choose the one in the middle, while the remaining people are equally divided, half choosing the most expensive and the others choosing the least expensive.

Comment on the importance of a salesperson giving his full, undivided attention to the prospect.

When you're in the presence of a prospect, he should be the single most important person in the world to you. Look him squarely in the eye and listen carefully to what he says. Don't insult him by letting your eyes wander.

Why did Baker go for a second and then a third suit after the first sale? Isn't this being greedy, and couldn't he have ended up with no sale?

A salesperson will never get a large order unless he asks for one. When you're in front of a receptive prospect, take advantage of the moment. Don't be so eager to get out the door and rush off to your next appointment —the next prospect might not even show up. Don't be afraid to push for a large order. In Baker's case, there was little risk that he would lose the first suit sale—and since he had much more to gain than to lose, his attempt to increase the order was an intelligent decision. It also required little effort as compared to approaching a new prospect.

Is it proper to attempt more than one close in a sales presentation!

If at first you don't succeed, try again—and again. Don't hesitate to close several times—more sales are closed on the second and subsequent attempts than on the first time around. It's even been said that the sale doesn't actually begin until the prospect says no!

Doesn't the prospect resent a salesperson's attempt to give two or more closes?

No, not when you have a soft-sale presentation. But people resent high-pressure tactics, so use finesse when you close a sale. People also resent the salesperson who doesn't know how to close a sale. Often, a prospect wants to buy, but the novice salesperson lacks the ability to show him how! He makes it easy for the prospect to "think it over." Procrastination causes frustration and is a disservice to the prospect. Part of your job as a salesperson is to *help* people buy—and this is best achieved when you close the sale.

How does one draw the line so that he or she won't appear to be high-pressure?

It's such a fine line that it *can't* be drawn. However, don't be overly concerned about coming across as high-pressure. Sometimes it's all right to put a little pressure on a prospect in order to force a decision—even if it's a no. Most important, however, is recognizing when you should "ease up," and this is something that you have to be able to sense.

Why can't a salesperson simply call back when a prospect wants to "think it over"? As a matter of courtesy, shouldn't the prospect's request be respected?

It's not discourteous to attempt to persuade a prospect to buy now even though he prefers to delay his decision. After all, it may be to his best interests. And yes, it's true that sometimes a person might feel uncomfortable about buying today—because he's an indecisive person. You must realize, however, that the longer the period of time that lapses *after* the presentation, the less are your chances of getting the order. Why? Because people aren't able to retain all the reasons why they *should* buy. Knowing this, many top salespersons have a now-or-never philosophy. But there are valid reasons why a salesperson should sometimes call back on a prospect. The difficult thing for most novice salespeople is sizing up prospects in order to determine which route to take—call back or close on the spot. Leading salespeople are able eventually to acquire a "sixth sense," and by carefully analyzing each of your sales presentations, the process of developing *your* sixth sense will be enhanced.

What do seasoned salespeople do about dealing with rejection?

First, it hurts even the best salespeople when they get rejected. Nobody likes it, but the seasoned salesperson understands that it's part of the business and learns to live with it. Above all, he doesn't take it as a personal rejection. Through his past experiences, he understands that the law of averages will work in his favor if he makes enough calls. He knows that so many calls equal so many sales. And when he doesn't make a sale, he doesn't become discouraged and carry it over to the next sales presentation.

Throughout Baker's close(s), he uses the minor-major closing technique. Please elaborate on how this works.

Major decisions are more difficult to make than minor ones. With this in mind, Baker gives the prospect a series of minor decisions to make. For example, it may be difficult for a person to make a $25,000 buying decision to purchase a new car. But, it's relatively simple to make a series of minor decisions affirmatively answering questions such as, "Do you want the four-door or the two-door?"; "Do you want it with white-walls?"; "Which color?"; "With or without power windows?"; and so on. In a minor-major close, the buyer is never asked the major question, "Are you going to buy?" That's always assumed. Note that assuming the sale and the minor-major close go hand in hand.

There are several times during Baker's presentation when the prospect indicates that he doesn't want to buy. Yet, Baker continues with his presentation.

Sometimes it's wise for a salesperson not to make an issue out of a prospect's resistance to buy. You don't want to make a mountain out of a molehill. Of course, if you keep hearing the same objection again and again, then it must be confronted head-on.

Is there anything wrong with letting the prospect know how much you want his business?

Never keep it a secret that you're there to do business with him. In fact, it's proper to say, "I want your business, and I'll give you so much service that you' wonder how you ever did business with anyone else. You may also ask, "What do I have to do to get you business?"

Why does Baker cross-examine the prospect in suc detail when asking him for referrals?

Because good prospecting is essential for all salespe sons. And referrals make excellent prospects. Baker very aggressive in his efforts to get referrals—becaus sometimes it's necessary to "pull" names out of peopl Never hesitate to ask your customers for referrals. An don't do it just on the initial sale—constantly ask f them. If you give them good service, your customer will be delighted to recommend people to you.

Please comment on a "canned" presentation.

A sales presentation repeated vertabim to every pro pect is not effective. First, it doesn't allow for flexibi ity; second, unless you're an excellent actor, the prospe will probably know that you're reciting it by memory In addition, such presentations generally lack enthus asm and conviction.

Is it recommended to continually change one's sale presentation because it doesn't always work on ever prospect?

While a sales presentation shouldn't be delivere verbatim, there must be some consistency in how yo sell. While you must be flexible and adapt your preser tation to each prospect, you must be careful to avoi changing it each time a sale doesn't result. Even with perfect sales presentation, you "can't sell 'em all."

Should a new sales trainee always "go by the book and do exactly what the company instructs him to do

Yes, as long as you're not asked to do anything that violates your principles. You must understand that your company wants you to succeed (it's in the company's best interest for you to do well), and you are trained according to what management believes works. You must assume that the company's management, with years of experience, knows more about the business than you, a beginner. With this in mind, you should do exactly as you're instructed; then, if you fail, it's *their* fault. But if you do it your way and fail, it's *your* fault. Often, salespeople recognize the value of their company's selling techniques only after they become seasoned. What didn't seem right at first, does after all! It's a mistake to "fight the system." Only after you have acquired enough success through personal experience and achievement should you begin to deviate from the company's proven way.

How can a salesperson "practice" his sales presentation?

Someone once said, "Only fishermen and salespeople ever practice." But salespeople *should* practice. Rehearsing one's presentation in between calls while driving is an effective way to use that time. Practicing in front of a mirror, a friend, or a spouse and using a tape-recorder and/or video-recorder are also helpful.

What are some good sources for a salesperson to seek to improve his or her selling skills?

Like other professionals (physicians, attorneys, accountants, architects, etc.), you must make it a lifetime practice to be a student of your vocation. Books and trade magazines are obvious sources for additional knowledge. And today, many audio and video tapes are available. Also, you should become active in various trade associations. Finally, one of the most overlooked sources is seeking out top salespeople for their advice—and "riding shotgun," observing in action. In general, most leading salespeople are flattered to be asked—and delighted to accommodate a fellow salesperson. What more, don't overlook asking salespeople in unrelated fields; selling ideas can be transferred from one industry to another.

If an individual does not succeed selling one particular product, is it advisable for him or her to seek nonselling career?

No. It shouldn't be assumed that an individual will not succeed in selling another product in another field. The important thing for a person to do is to find the "right" product that best matches his or her aptitude. For instance, a person without a technical aptitude might do poorly in the computer field but exceptionally well in the securities field. There are many success stories about salespeople who failed in one industry and went on to excel in another.

Is there a stereotyped personality that a salesperson must have in order to have a successful sales career?

Studies of top-producing salespersons indicate that no stereotypes exist. The fast-talking, extroverted salesperson is more myth than fact. While it is true that Ash and Rodgers are outgoing, dynamic individuals, Gandolfo, Hardeman, and Shafiroff are soft-spoken, and in a large group of salespeople they probably would not be identified as the number one producer in their respective fields. In fact, when first meeting them, they appear to be somewhat on the shy side. Perhaps this false first impression gives them a selling edge because prospects are caught off guard.

Possessing the God-given ability of a wonderful gift of gab is not what makes all five sales experts so outstanding (however, it is true that every salesperson must like people—selling is not for the introvert). The common denominators that make them so successful are our standing work habits, product knowledge, self-confidence, follow-through, conviction, and enthusiasm. The days are long gone when a salesperson could excel simply by possessing an outgoing personality. In truth, a successful sales career probably always required more substance.

In many instances, Ash, Gandolfo, Hardeman, Rodgers, and Shafiroff use similar selling techniques. In fact, in places, this book contains noticeable repetition. Please comment.

This repetition was intentionally included in the book. Why? Because it's important for the reader to realize that techniques that work when selling one product are applicable in unrelated industries. If you sell securities, for instance, it is hoped that you won't limit yourself to acquiring new ideas only from Shafiroff; the same holds true with the other four sales experts who appear in this book. Review how each of these five outstanding salespeople sell—then pick and choose the techniques that will work best for you. By doing so, you can vastly improve *your* sales presentation.

What is the best way to get the most benefit out of *The Perfect Sales Presentation*?

Read it several times—study it. This book contains a wealth of information, and even by incorporating only one new technique in your presentation you can substantially increase your earnings. However, don't limit yourself to one. . . .

ABOUT THE AUTHOR

ROBERT L. SHOOK is a former chairman of the board of a national sales organization. Currently he is a full-time writer, the author of more than twenty books, half of them on selling, including *The IBM Way*, coauthored with Buck Rodgers. He resides in Columbus, Ohio, with his wife and three children.

For 1990,

BANTAM MEANS BUSINESS!

**Turn the page for
a preview of the
newest business books
now available in
Bantam paperback
wherever you buy books.**

From:

THE PERFECT SALES PRESENTATION
by Robert L. Shook

Advice From:

MARY KAY ASH, Founder and Chairman of Mary Kay Cosmetics, Inc.

JOE GANDOLFO, The world's #1 life insurance agent

BETTYE C. HARDEMAN, America's #1 residential real estate agent

FRANCIS G. "BUCK" RODGERS, Marketing Consultant and former Vice President of worldwide marketing for IBM

MARTIN SHAFIROFF, Managing Director of Shearson/Lehman Brothers and the #1 stockbroker in the world

Mary Kay Ash believes that a salesperson gets only one chance to make a good first impression. For this reason, she thinks that the initial approach to a prospect is the most crucial part of the sales presentation. "All the selling skills in the world won't matter if you don't get your foot in the door," she claims.

The five sales experts agree that the way in which Baker immediately identifies himself to the prospect is professional and effective. "I like his directness," Hardeman says. "Up front, Baker states his name, the company he represents, and that it specializes in men's custom clothing. Unlike a lot of salesmen, he doesn't beat around the bush."

"He does what I used to do when I first got started in the insurance business." Gandolfo says. "I represented a company called Kennesaw Life Insurance Company, and after I'd introduce myself, I'd say, 'I'm sure you're familiar with Kennesaw Life.' Most people automatically nod their heads in agreement, especially when a salesperson's head is bobbing up and down. Now, I know that the vast majority of people never heard of the company, but by the way I said it, they thought they were *supposed* to know who Kennesaw was."

Gandolfo also likes Baker's appearance and the fact that he wears a Winchester suit. "It's a big mistake for a salesperson not to use the product he sells," the insurance agent states. "It's paramount to a Mercedes salesman driving a Caddy or a Chevy. Unless you believe in your product one hundred percent, you're simply not going to be effective. And I'll tell you something. Before I owned a million dollars of life insurance, I couldn't sell a million-dollar policy because I couldn't understand how anyone could afford so much coverage. Once I was insured for a million, and several more later on, I had the conviction to convince others that they, too, should be insured for those amounts. People sense this kind of conviction the very moment a salesman opens his mouth—whether he's in the same room or on the telephone."

Gandolfo, Shafiroff, and Rodgers are strong advocates of "concept selling" and like the way Baker tells the prospect, "I would like to share an idea with you." Gandolfo, for instance, initially tells a prospect, "I'm in the insurance and tax-shelter business, and I'm assuming that you pay more than four thousand dollars a year in taxes, personal or corporate. If so, you're paying too much and I'd like to run some ideas by you." This statement is a big attention-getter and opens the door with Gandolfo capturing immediate interest. "Who wouldn't be interested if they're paying more than four thousand a year in taxes?" he says. "Of course, I have to substantiate that statement in my presentation."

Likewise, in Shafiroff's initial approach he emphasizes that he deals in values. He stresses, "Wherever those values may be, and in whatever markets those values may be, my main concern is finding them for you. I also concentrate on special situations, seeking out companies with low multiples, high dividends, significant book values, and the possibility of realizing substantial capital gains." Shafiroff explains that he doesn't sell a specific stock during his first contact with a prospect. "I merely introduce myself and talk to him about my investment philosophy to see if it's in harmony with his. If we're not conceptually on the same wavelength, then I don't have anything to sell him."

Rodgers points out that the IBM cold-call approach creates initial interest by making a statement: "We're in the business of trying to provide solutions to a variety of different problems. Technology is moving very fast today, and I deal with many companies similar to yours, Mr. Prospect, where the use of our equipment has improved their profits. All we're trying to do at IBM is enhance productivity. For instance, our machines may accomplish this by enabling your volume to grow without having to increase your manpower. However, in order to take advantage of our equipment, there are a few things I have to know about your company." Then, soon into the presentation, a fact-finding session occurs.

During his initial approach, Baker mentions the names of several of his satisfied customers. This is done to establish credibility that his product has been well received by prominent people in the community. The five sales experts agree that this is an important procedure because it lets the prospect know that your product has benefited leading businesspersons who have good judgment. Shafiroff, who still makes it a practice to make six calls every day, claims that his best receptions are from those prospects referred to him by his existing clientele. When he mentions, "So-and-so told me to call you, Mr. Prospect," it's like having an introduction that gives him an immediate endorsement. The prospect knows that Shafiroff must have a fine reputation and expertise, because he respects the opinion of the third party.

From:

GET TO THE POINT: HOW TO SAY WHAT YOU MEAN AND GET WHAT YOU WANT
by Karen Berg and Andrew Gilman

The Three-Minute Presentation Writing Technique

Somebody once asked Abraham Lincoln how long it took him to prepare a speech. "It takes me about two weeks to write a good twenty-minute speech," he said, "but I can write a *forty*-minute speech in *one* week. And," he added, "I can give a two-hour talk on almost any subject right now." Or, as a correspondent of ours once put it: "If I'd had more time, I'd have written you a shorter letter."

The point? It's hard to be concise.

With our three-minute presentation writing technique, however, we give you a way to cut the job down to size. Once you are proficient with it, you should be able to draft your presentation in three minutes or less, regardless of length. Our technique works whether you make thirty-second, five-minute, or two-hour presentations.

The technique centers on two easy steps:

1. Stating your conclusion
2. Listing your arguments

These elements comprise the core of your presentation. Almost the entire structure flows from them. A third element is often necessary to complete the scheme, and that has to do with the "lead" we just mentioned. We'll discuss that later.

The first step is the key, but it rests on doing something that does *not* come naturally to most people. The natural tendency in formal communications seems to be to save the conclusion—recommendation, action plan, sales pitch—for the end. Our writing technique, however, reverses that process.

Step One. Make a succinct, one-, two-, or three-line statement of your message; the bottom line of your presentation.

By the time you're ready to start writing you should be able to do this fairly easily. If you can't, the chances are you're not ready to write.

This point of departure acts like a mental funnel, channeling your whole thought process into a tightly focused output. It makes for a stronger presentation because it forces you to focus on your *message* rather than your argument.

Case Study: A client of ours, a research scientist with a pharmaceutical firm, provides an excellent illustration of why this is so important. She came to us to improve her presentation skills following her first experience in presenting to senior business management.

True to the scientific method in which background and data precede the conclusion, our scientist launched into an hour's worth of data related to her projects. After about three minutes, the president of the company slammed his hand on the conference table and demanded, "Do we have a new drug here, or *don't* we?"

For him, this was the bottom line. If the answer was *yes*, then he wanted to hear the details; if it was *no*, the details were irrelevant. If it was *maybe*, he could decide, but without knowing the point of the message, a lengthy exposition was unacceptable.

The principle illustrated by this example is true even when it's not a go/no-go situation, as in the preceding case study. Look at it from a listener's point of view: When you know where an argument is leading, you can judge how well the points substantiate the conclusion as the argument unfolds.

In a sense, the facts that make up the argument are just packaging; they usually won't be remembered.

Another thing to consider is that in many informal presentation situations (in the hall, in the elevator) you may be cut off at any moment. Even in formal meetings you never know what key figure may have to leave early. So, whatever the circumstance, give them your message early.

Where to start. Begin. Grab a pad and a pencil; you're ready to start creating your presentation. First state your conclusion, your recommendation, and your action plan. Most often this should take the form of a direct call for action.

- "Lease a car from us. It will give you convenience, flexibility, and reliability."
- "I recommend that we reorganize our materials supply system and keep this plant open."
- "My committee's recommendation is that the management invest four-point-seven million dollars in this new line of business. We'd like your approval."

What's *your* conclusion? Write it down. Say it out loud. How does it sound to you? Make it clear and strong. You're off and running. Once your conclusion is set, the rest of your presentation should fall into place.

Step Two. List the selling points that support your conclusion.

These two elements—your *conclusion* and *action plan* and your list of *selling points*—form the backbone of your presentation. Here's how it works:

Conceptually, we divide presentations into three sections:

- Beginning
- Middle
- End

in which you:
- Tell 'em what you're gonna tell 'em
- Tell 'em
- Tell 'em what you told 'em

The beginning and ending essentially mirror each other, stating your conclusion and briefly summarizing the supporting material. The middle, the body of the presentation, consists of discussing that material in detail.

From:

PAY YOURSELF WHAT YOU'RE WORTH: HOW TO MAKE TERRIFIC MONEY IN DIRECT SALES
by Shirley Hutton and Constance deSwaan

Motivation and Goals

Don Bosson, a top division manager based in Joliet, Illinois and number one in the Fuller Brush company, is the quintessential committed salesman with strong values and valuable ideas about how to succeed in sales. He's been with the Fuller Brush company for nearly thirty years after a brief career as a luncheonette manager for W. T. Grant. He found his way to sales serendipitously.

"A friend told me he was selling for Fuller Brush and that it was a great thing to do. I thought I'd take a look at the business," he explained. "Since it was okay with the company for me to go out in the field with my friend. I did, and that clinched it. He was so *bad*—he did *everything* badly—that I thought, if this guy can make money selling door-to-door, so can I. As it turned out, I joined the company and he quit two months later."

Don excelled at sales and was promoted to field manager after two years, where he mostly recruited dealers. "At that time, twenty-four years ago, we just looked for men who wanted full-time sales jobs. It was company policy. Now that's all changed. We have mostly part-timers, and both men and women."

Over the years, he moved up to the top slot with Fuller Brush. What does he have that's special? How did he do it? What keeps him motivated? "It takes drive and desire. That's the start. You have to want to excel," he said. "When you excel, you think in terms of being a leader, not a follower. And if you want to be a leader, you'll be willing to put the effort forward that's good old-fashioned drive, to compete and be number one," he told me.

Don firmly believes that being a self-starter is "a must" in direct sales. However, many people will disagree with him. Though it's an asset to be a self-starter, many are not. They get their "push" through motivation by talking to or learning from others. Don felt differently and it worked for him. He advises. "Don't wait for someone to show you how to do anything. Just go and do it! Learn from your mistakes, but do it. Then do your best. It doesn't matter if you want the excitement that comes from the money or moving ahead. Take a chance on yourself."

These days, he's at his office at five-thirty or six in the morning, often putting in an eleven- or twelve-hour day. Don has made a lifetime commitment to his career, getting satisfaction from his achievements while still setting and meeting new goals.

Don and other outstanding direct sellers share an understanding of the qualities it takes to achieve: persistence, energy, enthusiasm, goal-setting, and being self-starting. No one has actually come up with a formula describing the ideally successful salesperson. The formula will always vary because each one of us is unique—not only in terms of our strengths and weaknesses, but because of timing, location, and what we want. Also, we all don't aspire to being number one or number ten (or even number one hundred) in a company.

But *why* we want to achieve is another matter—and an individual one. Many of us need and crave recognition, and approval. Others are content with the more tangible rewards—high income, jewelry, cars, overseas trips—and might even shy away from public attention. Still others labor long and hard working for work's sake—they're intimately involved in being productive, needing to accomplish as much as they can in a lifetime. And yet others appreciate and enjoy dollops of each—a little recognition, some money, the pleasure of spending a day doing what one *likes*.

The day you sign up with a direct sales company, you're automatically an enterpreneur. This means you are on your own, running your own "shop" in the manner that suits you best. It will operate by your own set of rules and goal-setting strategies, and of course there'll be changes to deal with and information to decipher. Each day will call for *effort* to keep going, especially when things look confusing or bleak. When you're an entrepreneur, you clock in and out at your chosen hours and your company operates almost entirely on *your own steam*! No boss will check up on you, there's no traveling to an office, and there's no gauranteed check on Fridays. The company you build at your desk reflects who you are and how you think. You decide the limits and how much money you'll earn. You've got to be *motivated*!

When you're an entrepreneur, you'll be taking a number of risks. Risk taking may reward you with *success* when your efforts pay off. But taking risks can also bring rejection, teasing, and discouragement. In tougher times, you must call on your stronger self, shrug off negativity, and believe you're worthy and that what you're doing is worthwhile. I bring this point up again because it's so critical to winning in sales—you've got to roll with the punches and be guided by the force of your high *self-esteem*!

Surprisingly, many people think their self-esteem is *lower* than it is. I've listened to thousands of stories over the years of successful women and men who joined the sale business originally believing they'd fail. Barbara Hammond, the Home Interiors vice president mentioned earlier, told me, "Sometimes I meet women who've signed up with us and I discover that we are the *only ones* to have ever encouraged them to achieve something for themselves," she said. "I found there are so few women who *believe* in themselves, or think they even *have* potential."

From:

CASHING IN ON THE AMERICAN DREAM: HOW TO RETIRE AT 35
by Paul Terhorst

Part 1 of this book reveals the formula that can turn your early retirement dream into a here-and-now reality. The formula has three parts. First, you'll find out how much money you need, how to invest, and how to spend. Next, you'll see how to kick the work habit. Finally, you'll get some ideas about what's out there and how to get started in your new life. Follow the formula and you'll never snooze through lukewarm coffee and bad cognac at your retirement dinner.

The rules you need to follow aren't conventional; neither is retiring after only ten or fifteen years of work. But they're simple rules, far more simple than the rules you've followed up to now. I've set out the rules in big block letters so you won't miss them. The three-part formula in part 1 is:

Do your arithmetic
Do some soul-searching
Do what you want

Part 2 expands on this formula. It tells how to make the formula come alive for you. It presents real-life case studies, tells how to save on taxes, looks at retiring with kids, and suggests a few lifestyle changes that can save hundreds of thousands of dollars. Someone once said it's not ideas that change things, but tactics. Part 2 of this book helps you come up with tactics that fit your style. All that's required on your part is a little imagination.

Later on, when you're 55 or 65, if you want to you can

"unretire" and go back to work. We used to work and then retire. This book suggests you work, then retire, then consider going back to work. Under this plan you devote your middle years to yourself and your family. During those years your mental and physical powers reach their height. You can explore, grow, and invest your time in what's most imporant to you. You can enjoy your children while they're still at home. Later, after you've lived the best years for yourself, you can go back to work if you want to. The choice will be up to you.

Pro athletes never plan forty-year careers. Martina Navratilova, Fernando Valenzuela, and Magic Johnson know their playing years are numbered. My work life lasted twelve years. To me, twelve years seems the minimum for a solid, proper career. But for football players, twelve years is the brilliant career of a superstar. Bob Griese, Herschel Walker, and Walter Payton may play twelve years. But most athletes burn out before they ever hit their Thirties Crisis. They may continue to dream of a chance to play in a Super Bowl, haggle over one more contract, or enjoy another headline. But their bodies scream at them to quit.

A tackle graduates from Ohio State and gets a signing bonus from the Raiders. For two years he draws a six-figure salary to play preseason games, beat up on special teams, and learn the playbook. In his third year he begins to start. Al Davis connects the name with the face, the fans and press talk about his quickness, and opposing players respect his talent. Our man plays three or four more years. During that period his salary doubles and then doubles again. He also makes big money on promotions and endorsements. But the travel, late nights, long workouts, mental strain, and injuries slow him by a fraction of a second. He begins to dread that inevitable Sunday when a younger player starts in his place. A season later he's washed up, as useless as a water boy without a pail.

But our man hired an agent to help him make deals, invest, and prepare for retirement. When his playing career ends he can live the rest of his life on interest and dividends from his investments. He may choose to buy a car dealership or open a saloon. But he may also choose to travel, relax on the beach, or organize a Special Olympics for retarded children.

We executives probably think we're smarter than the average jock. Most of us handle our own investments. But who's to tell *us* when to retire? Should we retire in our early 30s, like Sandy Koufax? In our 40s, like Pete Rose? Or in our 60s, like our fathers, grandfathers, and great-grandfathers? If a washed-up Raider can't decide to retire, Al Davis decides for him. Do you want your company to decide for you? Or do you want to step down on your own, with dignity, when you're still young and clearly in command?

This book is the first attempt to do for executives, screenwriters, models, stock jockeys, whiz kids, and mad marketeers what agents like Irving Marks do for highly paid jocks. Start thinking like athletes and you may wind up retiring at the same age they do. And you've got a big advantage. Their legs are shot. You can go back to work if you feel like it.